science for a changing world

Prepared in cooperation with the State of Vermont,
Vermont Geological Survey

Provisional Zircon and Monazite Uranium-Lead Geochronology for Selected Rocks From Vermont

By John N. Aleinikoff, Nicholas M. Ratcliffe, and Gregory J. Walsh

Open-File Report 2011–1309

U.S. Department of the Interior
U.S. Geological Survey

U.S. Department of the Interior
KEN SALAZAR, Secretary

U.S. Geological Survey
Marcia K. McNutt, Director

U.S. Geological Survey, Reston, Virginia: 2011

For more information on the USGS—the Federal source for science about the Earth,
its natural and living resources, natural hazards, and the environment:
World Wide Web: http://www.usgs.gov
Telephone: 1-888-ASK-USGS

For an overview of USGS information products, including maps, imagery, and publications,
visit http://www.usgs.gov/pubprod

To order this and other USGS information products, visit http://store.usgs.gov

Suggested citation:
Aleinikoff, J.N., Ratcliffe, N.M., and Walsh, G.J., 2011, Provisional zircon and monazite uranium-lead
geochronology for selected rocks from Vermont: U.S. Geological Survey Open-File Report 2011–1309,
46 p., available only online at http://pubs.usgs.gov/of/2011/1309/.

Contents

Figures

Tables

Conversion Factors

Multiply	By	To obtain
Length		
micrometer (μm)	0.00003937	inch (in.)
centimeter (cm)	0.3937	inch (in.)
millimeter (mm)	0.03937	inch (in.)
meter (m)	3.281	foot (ft)
kilometer (km)	0.6214	mile (mi)
Volume		
cubic meter (m^3)	35.31	cubic foot (ft^3)
Mass		
milligram (mg)	0.00003527	ounce, avoirdupois (oz)
gram (g)	0.03527	ounce, avoirdupois (oz)
kilogram (kg)	2.205	pound avoirdupois (lb)

Horizontal coordinate information is referenced to the World Geodetic System datum of 1984 (WGS 84).

Provisional Zircon and Monazite Uranium-Lead Geochronology for Selected Rocks From Vermont

By John N. Aleinikoff, Nicholas M. Ratcliffe, and Gregory J. Walsh

Introduction

This report presents the results of zircon uranium-lead (U-Pb) geochronologic analyses of 24 rock samples collected and analyzed in support of the "Bedrock Geologic Map of Vermont" by Ratcliffe and others (in press). The samples in this study were collected from mapped exposures identified while conducting either new, detailed (1:24,000-scale) geologic quadrangle mapping or reconnaissance mapping, both of which were used for compilation of the bedrock geologic map of Vermont. Nearly all of the collected samples were judged to be igneous rocks (either intrusive or extrusive) on the basis of field relations and geochemistry. The one exception is the Okemo Quartzite on Ludlow Mountain. Sampling rocks of uncertain origin was avoided as much as possible.

These geochronologic data were used to supplement regional correlations between igneous suites on the basis of similar geochemistry and geologic mapping. The locations of the sample sites and the assignment of the rocks to mapped igneous suites and their members are shown on the "Bedrock Geologic Map of Vermont." The geographic coordinates specifying the location of each sample are approximate and were either digitized from point locations shown on the 1:100,000-scale geologic map or located in reference to cultural features visible on satellite imagery (Google Earth). The coordinates were not obtained by a global positioning system (GPS) receiver.

Geochronology

Analytical Methods

Rock samples weighing approximately 10 kilograms (kg) were collected from outcrops in Vermont. After the rocks were crushed and pulverized, the material was processed over a Wilfley table to concentrate heavy minerals. Further processing included separating the iron-bearing minerals on a magnetic separator and concentrating those minerals with densities greater than about 3.3 g/cm^3 by sinking them in methylene iodide. Individual grains were handpicked using a binocular microscope, mounted in epoxy, ground to nearly half of their thickness to expose internal zones, and polished sequentially using 6-μm and 1-μm diamond suspension. All of the grains were imaged in transmitted and reflected light using a petrographic microscope and in cathodoluminescence (CL) using a scanning electron microscope (SEM).

Before 1993, zircon samples from Vermont, including four in this study, were dated by thermal ionization mass spectrometry (TIMS). Beginning in 1993, Vermont zircon samples, including 20 in this study, were dated using the sensitive high resolution ion microprobe

(SHRIMP). This work was performed using the U.S. Geological Survey/Stanford University SHRIMP-reverse geometry (SHRIMP–RG), SHRIMP II at the Research School of Earth Sciences (Australian National University, Canberra), or SHRIMP II at the Geological Survey of Canada.

The TIMS analytical procedures followed methods described in Aleinikoff and others (1996). The zircons were abraded (Krogh, 1982; Aleinikoff and others, 1990) to remove overgrowths and metamict areas. Next, the zircons were dissolved, and uranium and lead were extracted from the solution for isotopic analysis. In some cases, the material removed by abrasion (dust from an area referred to as the "rim" in the four TIMS concordia plots) was collected and analyzed separately in an attempt to determine the metamorphic age. Because subsequent CL imagery and SHRIMP analyses showed that many samples had multiple ages of metamorphic overgrowths, the TIMS analyses of this dust probably represented composite (or mixed) ages, which are likely to be geologically meaningless. Nonetheless, the data are shown for an historical perspective and to indicate that younger metamorphic rims were present in these samples. The data were reduced using the PBDAT program (Ludwig, 1991) and plotted using Isoplot 3 software (Ludwig, 2003). Three samples of zircon that were previously dated by TIMS (Ratcliffe and others, 1991) were subsequently re-analyzed by SHRIMP (tables 1, 2).

The SHRIMP analytical procedures followed the methods described by Williams (1998). The locations of the analytical spot (about 25 to 35 µm in diameter and about 1 µm in depth) were determined using (1) CL images to distinguish igneous cores and metamorphic overgrowths and (2) transmitted light images to avoid imperfections, such as cracks and inclusions. The crater was excavated using a primary oxygen beam of about 4 to 6 nanoamps (nA). A magnet cycled through the mass stations five times per analysis. Raw data were reduced using the Squid 1 program (Ludwig, 2001) or Squid 2 program (Kenneth R. Ludwig, Berkley Geochronology Laboratory, written commun., 2008) and plotted using Isoplot 3 software (Ludwig, 2003). The measured $^{206}Pb/^{238}U$ ages were referenced to zircon standard R33 (419±1 Ma; Black and others, 2004). The uranium concentrations were considered to be accurate to ±20 percent. U-Pb data were plotted on concordia plots to visually identify coherent age groups. For Precambrian samples that might have suffered minor lead loss, ages were determined by calculating a weighted average of selected $^{207}Pb/^{206}Pb$ ages; for Paleozoic samples, ages were determined by calculating a weighted average of selected $^{206}Pb/^{238}U$ ages. Plots of weighted average calculations are shown as insets with concordia plots. In some cases, concordant data sets permitted calculation of a concordia age (Ludwig, 1980, 1998), as noted on the figures.

Results

The U-Pb zircon geochronology results of 24 samples are presented chronologically from oldest to youngest. Information about the locations and lithologies of all samples is listed in table 1. Ages are summarized in table 2 and plotted in figures 1 through 24. SHRIMP isotopic data are listed in table 3; TIMS isotopic data are listed in table 4.

References Cited

Aleinikoff, J.N., Horton, J.W., Jr., and Walter, M., 1996, Middle Proterozoic age for the Montpelier Anorthosite, Goochland terrane, eastern Piedmont, Virginia: Geological Society of America Bulletin, v. 108, p. 1481–1491.

Aleinikoff, J.N., Schenck, W.S., Plank, M.O., Srogi, L., Fanning, C.M., Kamo, S.L., and Bosbyshell, H., 2006, Deciphering igneous and metamorphic events in high grade rocks of the Wilmington Complex, Delaware; Morphology, CL and BSE zoning, and SHRIMP U-Pb geochronology of zircon and monazite: Geological Society of America Bulletin, v. 118, p. 39–64.

Aleinikoff, J.N., Winegarden, D.L., and Walter, M., 1990, U-Pb ages of rims of zircons; A new analytical method using the air-abrasion technique: Chemical Geology (Isotope Geoscience Section), v. 80, p. 351–363.

Black, L.P., Kamo, S.L., Allen, C.M., Davis, D.W., Aleinikoff, J.N., Valley, J.W., Mundil, R., Campbell, I.H., Korsuch, R.J., Williams, I.S., and Foudoulis, C., 2004, Improved $^{206}Pb/^{238}U$ microprobe geochronology by the monitoring of a trace-element-related matrix effect; SHRIMP, ID–TIMS, ELA–ICP–MS and oxygen isotope documentation for a series of zircon standards: Chemical Geology, v. 205, p. 115–140.

Claoué-Long, J.C., Compston, W., Roberts, J., and Fanning, C.M., 1995, Two carboniferous ages; a comparison of SHRIMP zircon dating with conventional zircon ages and $^{40}Ar/^{39}Ar$ analysis, in Berggren, W.A., Kent, D.V., Aubrey, M.-P., and Hardenbol, J., eds., Geochronology time scales and global stratigraphic correlation: SEPM (Society for Sedimentary Geology) Special Publication 54, p. 3–21.

Krogh, T.E., 1982, Improved accuracy of U-Pb zircon ages by the creation of more concordant systems using an air abrasion technique: Geochimica et Cosmochimica Acta, v. 46, p. 485–494.

Ludwig, K.R., 1980, Calculation of uncertainties of U-Pb isotope data: Earth and Planetary Science Letters, v. 46, p. 212–220.

Ludwig, K.R., 1991, PBDAT—A computer program for processing Pb-U-Th isotope data, version 1.20: U.S. Geological Survey Open-File Report 88–542, 34 p.

Ludwig, K.R., 1998, On the treatment of concordant uranium-lead ages: Geochimica et Cosmochimica Acta, v. 62, p. 665–676.

Ludwig, K.R., 2001, Squid, version 1.05, A user's manual: Berkeley Geochronology Center Special Publication 2, 16 p.

Ludwig, K.R., 2003, Isoplot/Ex version 3.00, A geochronological toolkit for Microsoft Excel: Berkeley Geochronology Center Special Publication 4, 73 p.

Paces, J.B., and Miller J.D., Jr., 1993, Precise U-Pb ages of Duluth Complex and related mafic intrusions, northeastern Minnesota; Geochronological insights to physical, petrogenetic, paleomagnetic, and tectonomagmatic processes associated with the 1.1 Ga Midcontinent Rift System: Journal of Geophysical Research, v. 98, p. 13,997–14,013.

Ratcliffe, N.M., Aleinikoff, J.N., Burton, W.C., and Karabinos, P., 1991, Trondhjemitic, 1.35-1.31 Ga gneisses of the Mount Holly Complex of Vermont; Evidence for an Elzevirian event in the Grenville basement of the United States Appalachians: Canadian Journal of Earth Sciences, v. 28, p. 77–93

Ratcliffe, N.M., Stanley, R.S., Gale, M.H., Thompson, P.J., and Walsh, G.J., in press, Bedrock geologic map of Vermont: U.S. Geological Survey Scientific Investigations Map 3184, scale 1:100,000.

Richardson, C.H., 1924, The terranes of Bethel, Vermont, in Perkins, G.H., Fourteenth report of the State Geologist on the mineral industries and geology of Vermont, 1923–1924: Montpelier, Vt., Vermont Geological Survey, p. 77–103.

Stacey, J.S., and Kramers, J.D., 1975, Approximation of terrestrial lead isotope evolution by a two-stage model: Earth and Planetary Science Letters, v. 26, no. 2, p. 207–221.

Steiger, R.H., and Jäger, E., 1977, Subcommission on geochronology; Convention on the use of decay constants in geo- and cosmochronology: Earth and Planetary Science Letters, v. 36, p. 359–362.

Williams, I.S., 1998, U-Th-Pb geochronology by ion microprobe, *in* McKibben, M.A., Shanks, W.C., III, and Ridley, W.I., eds., Applications of microanalytical techniques to understanding mineralizing processes: Reviews in Economic Geology, v. 7, p. 1–35.

Williams, I.S., and Hergt, J.M., 2000, U-Pb dating of Tasmanian dolerites; a cautionary tale of SHRIMP analysis of high-U zircon, *in* Woodhead, J.D., Hergt, J.M., and Noble, W.P., eds., Beyond 2000; New frontiers in isotope geoscience, Abstracts and Proceedings, Lorne, Australia, January 30–February 4, 2000: Melbourne, Australia, University of Melbourne, p. 185–188.

Table 1. Locations of zircon samples collected for U-Pb geochronology in support of the "Bedrock Geologic Map of Vermont" (Ratcliffe and others, in press).

Sample number[1]	Field number	Map unit	Map sheet[2]	Description
1	Lon–1–A	Y^1dg	Southern	Hornblende diorite gneiss at South Londonderry.
2	VT–CSTR–1	Y^1bm	Southern	Baileys Mills tonalite gneiss in the Chester dome.
3	VT/Pe 1–88 (6327)	Y^1rt	Southern	Rawsonville trondhjemite gneiss at Bromley Mountain.
4	C718	Y^1fga	Southern	Felchville Gneiss (aplite facies) at Cavendish Gorge.
5	C609	Y^1fg	Southern	Felchville Gneiss (trondhjemite facies) at Felchville.
6B	VT/Pe 2–88 (6329)	Y^2bv	Southern	Bondville metadacite at Winhall River bridge.
7	87Rat–1 (3016A)	Y^2cp	Southern	Cole Pond tonalite gneiss.
8	VT/Ja 1–88	Y^2mig	Southern	Migmatite gneiss at Stratton Mountain.
9	VT/Lu 1-91	Y^2lgg	Southern	Fine-grained granodiorite of the Ludlow Mountain granodiorite gneiss at Okemo Mountain.
10	VT/Lu 2–91	Y^2lq	Southern	Okemo Quartzite—Detrital zircon.
11	87Rat–2	Y^2ch	Southern	College Hill Granite Gneiss at Stratton Mountain, which crosscuts older and deformed intrusive rocks and paragneiss.
12	VT/Lo 1–89	Y^2gg	Southern	Granitic gneiss, which crosscuts older and deformed intrusive rocks (suite ranging in age from 1.3 to 1.4 Ga) and paragneiss.
13	MC6000	$Y^{3A}mb$	Southern	Megacrystic augen gneiss at Brandon Gap.
16	R2008	$Y^{3B}p$	Southern	Migmatite gneiss in Pine Hill slice.
22	VT/Br 2–89	Onnt	Southern	Newfane tonalite intrudes Cram Hill Formation near South Newfane.
23	L–18	Onb	Southern	Trondhjemite in Barnard Gneiss proper (of Richardson, 1924) north of Proctorsville.
24	SR3053	Ont	Southern	Tonalite gneiss in the North River Igneous Suite near Bartonsville.
25	SP450	Ochv	Southern	Felsic volcanic layer interlayered with mafic volcanic rocks in Cram Hill Formation at Springfield.
38	MC3432	Sbg	Northern	Granite in the Braintree Intrusive Complex.
39	VT–Nq–1–97	Snd	Northern	Trondhjemite of Newport Intrusive Complex.
46	VT–CSTR–2	Dg	Southern	Granite in the Chester dome.
47	Barre#2	Dbbg	Northern	Barre Granite.
48	VT/Br 1–89	Dbmg	Southern	Black Mountain pluton.
49	VT/Pl 2–91	Dg	Southern	Granite dike south of Plymouth.

[1]The sample numbers correspond to numbers shown on the "Bedrock Geologic Map of Vermont" (Ratcliffe and others, in press).

[2]The "Bedrock Geologic Map of Vermont" (Ratcliffe and others, in press) is divided into northern and southern map sheets at latitude 43°52'30"N.

Table 2. Summary of analytical information and ages of samples from Vermont.

[See table 1 for locations. Ma, millions of years (mega-annum); NA, not applicable; ≈, approximately]

Sample number	Field number	Date analyzed	Instrument[1]	Mineral standard[2]	Mount number	Age and error (2σ) (Ma)	Method of age analysis[3]
1	Lon–1–A	1/4/2001	USGS–RG	R33	A133	1,393±9	76
2	VT–CSTR–1	4/25/1998	RSES SII	AS3	A105	1,383±13	76
3	VT/Pe 1–88 (6327)	10/11/1998	RSES SII	AS3	A102	1,367±16	76
4	C718	4/28/2009	GSC SII	R33	A342	1,372±11	76
5	C609	4/29/2009	GSC SII	R33	A342	1,370±11	76
6B	VT/Pe 2–88 (6329)	1989	TIMS	NA	NA	≈1,342	76
7	87Rat–1 (3016A)	10/11/1998	RSES SII	AS3	A102	1,321±9	76
8	VT/Ja 1–88	11/11/1999	USGS–RG	AS57	A117	1,326±4	76
9	VT/Lu 1–91	4/25/1996	RSES SII	SL13	Z2548	1,309±6	76
10	VT/Lu 2–91	1/4/2001	USGS–RG	R33	A133	1,261±62 to 1,359±32	dz
11	87Rat–2	1988	TIMS	NA	NA	1,244±8	76
12	VT/Lo 1–89	1988	TIMS	NA	NA	1,221±4	UI
13	MC6000	4/24/1998	RSES SII	AS3	A112	1,149±8	CA
16	R2008	4/24/1998	RSES SII	AS3	A105	1,037±6	CA
22	VT/Br 2–89	9/2/1999	USGS–RG	AS57	A115	502±4	68
23	L–18	11/19/1996	RSES SII	AS3	Z2727	496±8	68
24	SR3053	1996	TIMS	NA	NA	486±3	76
25	SP450	4/28/1997	RSES SII	AS3	Z2848	483±3	68
38	MC3432	1/3/2001	USGS–RG	R33	A133	421±7	CA
39	VT–Nq–1–97	3/22/2010	USGS–RG	R33	A354	425±3	68
46	VT–CSTR–2	11/12/1999	USGS–RG	AS57	A117	392±6	68
47	Barre#2	9/13/2000	USGS–RG	R33	A119	368±4	68
48	VT/Br 1–89z	9/14/2000	USGS–RG	R33	A119	364±4	68+76
48	VT/Br 1–89m	10/15/2011	USGS–RG	44069	A131	363±2	CA
49	VT/Pl 2–91	9/13/2000	USGS–RG	R33	A119	365±5	68

[1]Ion microprobe or other instrument used:

USGS–RG, U.S. Geological Survey/Stanford sensitive high resolution ion microprobe–reverse geometry (SHRIMP–RG).

RSES SII, Research School of Earth Sciences, Australian National University sensitive high resolution ion microprobe II (SHRIMP II).

GSC SII, Geological Survey of Canada SHRIMP II.

TIMS, thermal ionization mass spectrometry.

Table 2. Summary of analytical information and ages of samples from Vermont.—Continued

[2]Mineral standard used:

Zircon

R33, from monzodiorite of the Braintree Intrusive Complex, Vermont; 419±1 Ma (Black and others, 2004). Used since September 2000.

AS57, from gabbroic anorthosite, Duluth Complex, Minnesota; presumed age of 1,099±1 Ma (Paces and Miller, 1993). Used from September 1999 to January 2000.

AS3, from gabbroic anorthosite, Duluth Complex, Minnesota; 1,099±1 Ma (Paces and Miller, 1993). Used from November 1996 to May 1999.

SL13, Neoproterozoic zircon megacryst from stream gravels, Sri Lanka; 572 Ma (Claoué-Long and others, 1995; and Black and others, 2004). Used from February 1993 to July 1996.

Monazite

44069, from Wissahickon Schist, Yorklyn, Delaware; 424.9±0.4Ma (Aleinikoff and others, 2006).

[3]Age calculation method used:

76, weighted average of ^{207}Pb/^{206}Pb ages.

UI, upper intercept age.

CA, concordia age (Ludwig, 1980, 1998).

68, weighted average of ^{206}Pb/^{238}U ages.

dz, detrital zircon (individual grain ages only).

Table 3. Sensitive high resolution ion microprobe (SHRIMP) uranium-thorium-lead (U-Th-Pb) data for zircon and monazite from rocks of Vermont.

[Abbreviations are as follows: Ma, millions of years (mega-annum); NA, not applicable; ppm, parts per million; —, measured ^{204}Pb below detection limit; ρ, error correlation]

Analysis[1]	Measured ^{204}Pb/^{206}Pb	Measured ^{207}Pb/^{206}Pb	Percent common ^{206}Pb	Uranium (ppm)	Th/U	^{206}Pb/^{238}U (Ma)[2]	Error (Ma)[3]	^{207}Pb/^{206}Pb (Ma)[2]	Error (Ma)[3]	^{207}Pb/^{235}U[4]	Error (percent)[3]	^{206}Pb/^{238}U[4]	Error (percent)[3]	ρ
						Lon-1-A (Hornblende diorite gneiss at South Londonderry)								
Lon-1-A-1	0.000017	.0896	0.03	383	0.71	1,327.0	13.3	1,413	15	2.83	1.3	.2296	1.0	.799
Lon-1-A-2	—	.0848	0.00	399	0.62	1,274.9	12.8	1,311	15	2.56	1.3	.2191	1.0	.801
Lon-1-A-3	—	.0886	0.00	391	0.76	1,413.8	14.2	1,395	14	2.99	1.3	.2450	1.0	.810
Lon-1-A-4	—	.0890	0.00	592	0.82	1,386.9	13.7	1,404	12	2.95	1.2	.2403	1.0	.861
Lon-1-A-5	0.000008	.0887	0.01	712	1.07	1,394.6	13.7	1,396	10	2.95	1.2	.2415	1.0	.881
Lon-1-A-6	—	.0879	0.00	840	1.22	1,162.7	12.8	1,381	12	2.42	1.3	.1998	1.1	.885
Lon-1-A-7	0.000331	.0884	0.55	94	0.25	1,249.9	14.4	1,287	58	2.48	3.2	.2144	1.2	.369
Lon-1-A-8	0.000075	.0889	0.12	108	0.31	1,345.5	15.1	1,380	30	2.82	1.9	.2325	1.2	.600
Lon-1-A-9	0.000038	.0896	0.06	180	0.36	1,432.9	15.1	1,405	22	3.05	1.6	.2485	1.1	.693
Lon-1-A-10	0.000032	.0876	0.05	471	0.70	1,318.2	13.1	1,363	17	2.73	1.4	.2274	1.0	.753
Lon-1-A-11	—	.0890	0.00	721	1.34	1,405.4	13.9	1,405	10	2.99	1.2	.2436	1.0	.883
Lon-1-A-12	0.000007	.0882	0.01	825	1.49	1,411.6	13.8	1,385	10	2.97	1.1	.2444	1.0	.892
Lon-1-A-13	0.000055	.0901	0.09	502	1.39	1,387.1	13.8	1,411	13	2.96	1.2	.2404	1.0	.825
Lon-1-A-14	0.000017	.0875	0.03	372	0.57	1,362.4	13.7	1,366	15	2.83	1.3	.2354	1.0	.797
Lon-1-A-15	0.000068	.0891	0.11	255	0.33	1,393.8	14.6	1,387	22	2.93	1.6	.2413	1.1	.686
						VT-CSTR-1 (Baileys Mill tonalitic gneiss in Chester dome)								
VT-CSTR-1-1.1	0.000239	.0866	0.09	51	0.28	1,334.7	40.0	1,275	51	2.63	4.1	.2293	3.1	.767
VT-CSTR-1-1.2	0.000036	.0854	-0.01	426	0.08	1,328.2	27.9	1,314	12	2.68	2.3	.2286	2.2	.962
VT-CSTR-1-2.1	0.000022	.0890	-0.22	222	0.29	1,442.7	30.7	1,396	15	3.06	2.3	.2502	2.2	.939
VT-CSTR-1-2.2	0.000073	.0892	-0.41	87	0.28	1,482.5	33.0	1,386	24	3.13	2.6	.2572	2.3	.879
VT-CSTR-1-2.3	0.000062	.0787	-0.16	586	0.00	1,197.8	22.3	1,141	13	2.18	2.0	.2036	1.9	.944
VT-CSTR-1-3.1	-0.000040	.0885	-0.07	266	0.43	1,406.1	28.7	1,405	20	2.99	2.4	.2437	2.1	.895
VT-CSTR-1-4.1	0.000103	.0861	0.51	240	0.27	1,238.7	27.0	1,307	21	2.48	2.5	.2126	2.3	.902
VT-CSTR-1-4.2	-0.000016	.0820	0.19	616	0.05	1,206.8	25.5	1,250	16	2.34	2.3	.2063	2.2	.940
VT-CSTR-1-5.1	-0.000092	.0902	0.16	55	0.27	1,400.8	31.7	1,457	34	3.07	2.9	.2435	2.3	.798
VT-CSTR-1-5.2	0.000062	.0798	0.83	409	0.01	1,007.9	23.4	1,169	16	1.85	2.5	.1705	2.4	.946
VT-CSTR-1-6.1	0.000047	.0854	0.60	49	0.33	1,203.4	27.4	1,309	37	2.41	3.0	.2063	2.4	.775
VT-CSTR-1-6.2	0.000004	.0844	0.05	939	0.12	1,293.2	23.9	1,301	13	2.59	2.0	.2222	1.9	.940
VT-CSTR-1-6.3	-0.000085	.0873	0.27	131	0.28	1,315.7	26.4	1,393	29	2.77	2.6	.2273	2.1	.809
VT-CSTR-1-7.1	0.000044	.0764	0.51	859	0.02	992.2	23.6	1,090	12	1.75	2.5	.1671	2.5	.974
VT-CSTR-1-7.2	0.000060	.0881	-0.06	200	0.43	1,395.8	32.0	1,367	17	2.90	2.5	.2414	2.4	.939
VT-CSTR-1-8.1	0.006176	.2050	13.10	62	0.27	1,476.8	70.7	1,987	228	4.49	13.7	.2667	4.8	.348
VT-CSTR-1-8.2	-0.000263	.0915	0.62	61	0.53	1,343.0	32.8	1,531	60	3.07	4.1	.2341	2.5	.620
VT-CSTR-1-9.1	0.000857	.1002	1.74	80	0.33	1,323.3	28.0	1,387	90	2.78	5.2	.2286	2.2	.430

Table 3. Sensitve high resolution ion microprobe (SHRIMP) uranium-thorium-lead (U-Th-Pb) data for zircon and monazite from rocks of Vermont.—Continued

[Abbreviations are as follows: Ma, millions of years (mega-annum); NA, not applicable; ppm, parts per million; —, measured [204]Pb below detection limit; ρ, error correlation]

Analysis[1]	Measured [204]Pb/[206]Pb	Measured [207]Pb/[206]Pb	Percent common [206]Pb	Uranium (ppm)	Th/U	[206]Pb/[238]U (Ma)[2]	Error (Ma)[3]	[207]Pb/[206]Pb (Ma)[2]	Error (Ma)[3]	[207]Pb/[235]U[4]	Error (percent)[3]	[206]Pb/[238]U[4]	Error (percent)[3]	ρ
				VT–CSTR–1 (Baileys Mill tonalitic gneiss in Chester dome)—Continued										
VT–CSTR–1–9.2	-0.000053	.0885	-0.06	137	0.39	1,404.8	31.0	1,409	20	3.00	2.5	.2435	2.3	.907
VT–CSTR–1–10.1	0.000071	.0880	-0.15	334	0.31	1,411.2	27.2	1,361	14	2.93	2.1	.2441	2.0	.943
VT–CSTR–1–11.1	-0.000012	.0870	0.29	179	0.39	1,304.6	35.6	1,364	17	2.70	3.0	.2250	2.8	.952
VT–CSTR–1–12.1	0.000013	.0890	0.09	128	0.27	1,387.8	27.7	1,400	22	2.94	2.4	.2404	2.1	.873
VT–CSTR–1–12.2	0.000005	.0894	-0.06	237	0.22	1,422.3	33.1	1,410	16	3.04	2.6	.2467	2.4	.942
VT–CSTR–1–13.1	-0.000017	.0841	0.00	600	0.07	1,293.5	28.0	1,300	11	2.58	2.3	.2223	2.2	.969
VT–CSTR–1–14.1	0.000045	.0877	-0.06	100	0.28	1,388.3	32.6	1,363	26	2.88	2.8	.2400	2.4	.876
VT–CSTR–1–15.1	0.000006	.0754	0.08	842	0.03	1,062.2	21.2	1,077	11	1.86	2.1	.1792	2.1	.969
VT–CSTR–1–15.2	0.000281	.0865	0.44	40	0.45	1,264.1	35.6	1,259	66	2.47	4.5	.2166	2.9	.655
VT–CSTR–1–15.3	0.000046	.0892	-0.19	144	0.32	1,443.4	31.2	1,394	22	3.06	2.5	.2503	2.2	.886
VT–CSTR–1–16.1	-0.000020	.0865	-0.04	513	0.15	1,355.1	25.4	1,355	14	2.80	2.1	.2339	1.9	.935
VT–CSTR–1–16.2	-0.000196	.0895	0.00	61	0.34	1,414.7	31.1	1,472	37	3.13	3.0	.2462	2.3	.761
VT–CSTR–1–16.3	0.000043	.0893	0.01	660	0.16	1,408.3	34.3	1,397	28	2.98	2.9	.2440	2.5	.866
VT–CSTR–1–17.1	0.000008	.0846	0.33	1,542	0.11	1,239.6	27.9	1,303	28	2.48	2.7	.2127	2.3	.853
				VT/Pe 1–88 (6327) (Rawsonville trondhjemite gneiss at Bromley Mountain)										
VT/Pe–1–1.1	0.000043	.0876	0.07	111	0.22	1,392.8	19.6	1,361	13	2.89	1.6	.2408	1.5	.902
VT/Pe–1–2.1	0.000070	.0892	0.11	113	0.40	1,386.4	19.5	1,387	16	2.92	1.7	.2399	1.5	.874
VT/Pe–1–3.1	0.000112	.0889	0.18	206	0.36	1,398.4	19.2	1,367	19	2.91	1.7	.2418	1.4	.822
VT/Pe–1–4.1	0.000139	.0878	0.23	82	0.26	1,385.3	29.8	1,334	35	2.83	2.9	.2391	2.2	.773
VT/Pe–1–5.1	0.000056	.0877	0.09	179	0.34	1,406.3	19.6	1,358	22	2.91	1.8	.2431	1.4	.790
VT/Pe–1–6.1	0.000135	.0836	0.22	87	0.28	1,256.6	18.0	1,239	23	2.42	1.9	.2150	1.5	.789
				C718 (Felchville Gneiss (aplite facies) at Cavendish Gorge)										
C718–1.1	0.000064	.0887	0.104	130	0.34	1,342	22	1,378	17	2.81	1.9	0.232	1.7	0.89
C718–2.1	0.000103	.0893	0.169	113	0.32	1,378	25	1,379	23	2.89	2.2	0.238	1.9	0.84
C718–3.1	0.000060	.0897	0.098	209	0.45	1,404	24	1,402	17	2.98	2.0	0.243	1.7	0.89
C718–3.2	0.000879	.0762	1.543	362	0.02	1,080	17	725	79	1.57	4.1	0.180	1.7	0.42
C718–4.1	0.000135	.0882	0.223	94	0.24	1,368	26	1,345	28	2.81	2.5	0.236	2.0	0.81
C718–5.1	0.000066	.0876	0.109	110	0.29	1,414	25	1,353	21	2.92	2.2	0.244	1.9	0.86
C718–6.1	0.000079	.0884	0.130	199	0.29	1,370	22	1,368	16	2.85	1.9	0.237	1.7	0.90
C718–7.1	0.000103	.0893	0.168	88	0.36	1,410	27	1,379	25	2.96	2.4	0.244	2.0	0.83
C718–8.1	0.000021	.0842	0.035	321	0.06	1,266	19	1,291	11	2.52	1.7	0.217	1.6	0.94
C718–10.1	-0.000020	.0910	-0.032	101	0.36	1,353	25	1,452	20	2.95	2.2	0.235	1.9	0.88
C718–10.2	0.000016	.0750	0.027	1,731	0.00	980	14	1,062	6	1.70	1.5	0.165	1.4	0.98
C718–11.1	0.000065	.0875	0.107	88	0.23	1,369	25	1,351	21	2.82	2.2	0.236	1.9	0.86

Table 3. Sensitive high resolution ion microprobe (SHRIMP) uranium-thorium-lead (U-Th-Pb) data for zircon and monazite from rocks of Vermont.—Continued

[Abbreviations are as follows: Ma, millions of years (mega-annum); NA, not applicable; ppm, parts per million; —, measured 204Pb below detection limit; ρ, error correlation]

Analysis[1]	Measured 204Pb/206Pb	Measured 207Pb/206Pb	Percent common 206Pb	Uranium (ppm)	Th/U	206Pb/238U (Ma)[2]	Error (Ma)[3]	207Pb/206Pb (Ma)[2]	Error (Ma)[3]	207Pb/235U[4]	Error (percent)[3]	206Pb/238U[4]	Error (percent)[3]	ρ
				C718 (Felchville Gneiss (aplite facies) at Cavendish Gorge)—Continued										
C718–12.1	0.000043	.0878	0.070	151	0.35	1,370	25	1,366	23	2.85	2.2	0.237	1.9	0.85
C718–13.1	0.000015	.0904	0.025	123	0.30	1,395	25	1,428	18	3.01	2.0	0.242	1.8	0.89
C718–14.1	0.000042	.0872	0.069	128	0.45	1,381	24	1,353	19	2.85	2.0	0.238	1.8	0.88
C718–15.1	0.000051	.0880	0.083	88	0.26	1,328	24	1,367	21	2.76	2.2	0.229	1.9	0.87
C718–16.1	0.000118	.0884	0.195	101	0.27	1,326	27	1,355	31	2.74	2.6	0.229	2.1	0.79
C718–1.2	0.000034	.0765	0.057	784	0.01	1,107	16	1,095	8	1.96	1.5	0.187	1.5	0.97
C718–16.2	0.000063	.0774	0.106	459	0.03	1,109	16	1,109	11	1.98	1.6	0.188	1.5	0.94
C718–17.1	0.000482	.0874	0.805	40	0.27	1,267	28	1,211	60	2.41	3.8	0.217	2.3	0.60
C718–17.2	0.000145	.0904	0.237	75	0.25	1,416	26	1,390	24	2.99	2.3	0.245	1.9	0.84
C718–18.1	0.000285	.0860	0.473	36	0.34	1,340	30	1,244	126	2.60	6.8	0.230	2.3	0.34
C718–18.2	-0.000024	.0903	-0.039	151	0.47	1,435	23	1,440	13	3.12	1.8	0.249	1.7	0.93
				C609 (Felchville Gneiss (trondhjemite facies) at Felchville)										
C609–1.1	0.000048	.0869	0.079	259	0.17	1,299	20	1,343	11	2.66	1.7	0.224	1.6	0.94
C609–2.1	0.000015	.0880	0.025	149	0.36	1,334	21	1,377	13	2.79	1.8	0.230	1.7	0.93
C609–3.1	0.000097	.0884	0.159	133	0.34	1,298	21	1,362	16	2.69	1.9	0.224	1.7	0.89
C609–4.1	0.000036	.0881	0.059	125	0.38	1,365	23	1,373	66	2.85	3.8	0.236	1.7	0.44
C609–5.1	0.000069	.0892	0.113	143	0.49	1,351	22	1,388	15	2.84	1.8	0.234	1.7	0.90
C609–6.2	0.000033	.0878	0.054	303	0.24	1,339	20	1,368	10	2.78	1.6	0.231	1.6	0.94
C609–7.1	0.000026	.0883	0.043	99	0.37	1,323	23	1,380	17	2.77	2.0	0.229	1.8	0.89
C609–8.1	0.000043	.0881	0.070	145	0.43	1,377	23	1,372	56	2.87	3.4	0.238	1.7	0.50
C609–9.2	0.000041	.0880	0.067	166	0.48	1,357	22	1,370	14	2.83	1.8	0.234	1.7	0.92
C609–10.1	-0.000009	.0894	-0.014	160	0.52	1,384	22	1,415	13	2.96	1.8	0.240	1.7	0.92
C609–11.1	0.000039	.0888	0.064	136	0.45	1,386	23	1,388	15	2.92	1.9	0.240	1.7	0.91
C609–12.1	0.000017	.0889	0.028	160	0.40	1,390	23	1,396	14	2.94	1.8	0.241	1.7	0.92
C609–13.1	0.000033	.0845	0.055	188	0.11	1,248	20	1,292	14	2.48	1.8	0.214	1.7	0.91
C609–14.1	0.000048	.0867	0.078	161	0.39	1,389	24	1,339	21	2.85	2.1	0.240	1.8	0.85
C609–15.1	0.000064	.0896	0.105	117	0.27	1,395	25	1,398	18	2.96	2.1	0.242	1.8	0.89
C609–16.1	0.000074	.0877	0.122	197	0.31	1,410	23	1,352	77	2.91	4.3	0.244	1.7	0.38
C609–17.1	0.000061	.0898	0.100	138	0.36	1,394	24	1,403	18	2.96	2.0	0.242	1.8	0.89
C609–6.1	0.002524	.0795	4.720	199	0.01	498	9	-222	424	0.46	17.0	0.079	2.0	0.12
C609–9.1	0.000064	.0658	0.111	1,051	0.03	694	10	770	11	1.02	1.6	0.114	1.5	0.94
C609–16.2	0.000270	.0785	0.458	399	0.02	1,006	15	1,060	19	1.74	1.8	0.169	1.5	0.85
C609–17.1	0.000069	.0863	0.114	163	0.40	1,310	21	1,323	16	2.65	1.9	0.225	1.7	0.90
C609–17.2	0.000052	.0877	0.086	204	0.19	1,328	21	1,360	14	2.75	1.8	0.229	1.6	0.92

Table 3. Sensitive high resolution ion microprobe (SHRIMP) uranium-thorium-lead (U-Th-Pb) data for zircon and monazite from rocks of Vermont.—Continued

[Abbreviations are as follows: Ma, millions of years (mega-annum); NA, not applicable; ppm, parts per million; —, measured ^{204}Pb below detection limit; ρ, error correlation]

Analysis[1]	Measured ^{204}Pb/^{206}Pb	Measured ^{207}Pb/^{206}Pb	Percent common ^{206}Pb	Uranium (ppm)	Th/U	^{206}Pb/^{238}U (Ma)[2]	Error (Ma)[3]	^{207}Pb/^{206}Pb (Ma)[2]	Error (Ma)[3]	^{207}Pb/^{235}U[4]	Error (percent)[3]	^{206}Pb/^{238}U[4]	Error (percent)[3]	ρ
87Rat-1 (3016A) (Cole Pond tonalite gneiss)														
87Rat-1–1.1	-0.000051	.0872	-0.08	104	0.70	1,255.5	17.8	1,380	15	2.62	1.7	.2164	1.5	.880
87Rat-1–1.2	0.000023	.0823	0.04	541	0.14	1,228.5	16.5	1,245	9	2.38	1.5	.2101	1.4	.948
87Rat-1–2.1	0.000158	.0851	0.26	112	0.61	1,301.3	18.4	1,266	21	2.55	1.8	.2233	1.5	.813
87Rat-1–2.2	0.000028	.0780	0.05	663	0.00	1,189.9	15.9	1,137	7	2.16	1.4	.2022	1.4	.972
87Rat-1–3.1	0.000076	.0869	0.12	125	0.76	1,309.3	18.4	1,335	19	2.67	1.8	.2255	1.5	.833
87Rat-1–4.1	0.000080	.0860	0.13	97	0.51	1,302.0	18.9	1,313	19	2.62	1.8	.2239	1.5	.842
87Rat-1–4.2	0.000153	.0871	0.25	376	0.35	1,329.4	17.9	1,314	9	2.68	1.5	.2288	1.4	.944
87Rat-1–5.1	0.000036	.0868	0.06	62	0.53	1,329.4	19.7	1,344	22	2.73	1.9	.2292	1.5	.798
87Rat-1–5.2	0.000034	.0859	0.06	285	0.34	1,299.1	17.6	1,325	8	2.63	1.5	.2236	1.4	.955
87Rat-1–1.3	0.003050	.1259	5.06	45	0.39	1,299.1	25.0	1,267	339	2.55	17.5	.2229	2.1	.118
87Rat-1–6.1	0.000105	.0861	0.17	76	0.42	1,320.4	19.2	1,306	27	2.65	2.1	.2272	1.5	.735
87Rat-1–6.2	0.000487	.0874	0.81	56	0.41	1,345.1	20.1	1,210	40	2.56	2.5	.2304	1.6	.612
87Rat-1–7.1	0.000335	.0891	0.55	113	0.73	1,299.8	18.5	1,302	24	2.60	1.9	.2234	1.5	.767
87Rat-1–7.2	0.000032	.0852	0.05	300	0.35	1,313.0	17.8	1,311	9	2.64	1.5	.2259	1.4	.947
87Rat-1–8.1	0.000051	.0862	0.08	94	0.71	1,329.7	19.0	1,326	19	2.70	1.8	.2290	1.5	.831
87Rat-1–8.2	0.000022	.0855	0.04	239	0.29	1,346.3	18.3	1,320	9	2.73	1.5	.2319	1.4	.951
87Rat-1–9.1	0.000010	.0862	0.02	102	0.40	1,330.1	18.9	1,340	13	2.72	1.6	.2293	1.5	.915
87Rat-1–9.2	0.000425	.0841	0.71	301	0.11	1,099.8	14.8	1,149	18	2.01	1.7	.1864	1.4	.837
87Rat-1–10.1	0.000272	.0881	0.45	46	0.40	1,313.1	20.1	1,300	53	2.62	3.2	.2258	1.6	.508
87Rat-1–11.1	0.000098	.0864	0.16	134	0.70	1,351.7	18.8	1,316	14	2.73	1.6	.2329	1.5	.890
87Rat-1–11.2	0.000062	.0871	0.10	61	0.38	1,309.1	19.8	1,343	23	2.68	2.0	.2256	1.6	.795
87Rat-1–12.1	0.000093	.0856	0.15	101	0.63	1,291.6	18.2	1,300	17	2.58	1.7	.2219	1.5	.861
87Rat-1–13.1	0.000065	.0872	0.11	54	0.44	1,336.7	19.8	1,344	22	2.74	1.9	.2305	1.5	.808
87Rat-1–13.2	0.000007	.0855	0.01	270	0.36	1,363.5	18.5	1,325	10	2.77	1.5	.2351	1.4	.935
87Rat-1–14.1	0.000017	.0846	0.03	201	0.34	1,299.7	17.8	1,300	10	2.60	1.5	.2234	1.4	.939
VT/Ja 1–88 (Migmatite gneiss at Stratton Mountain)														
VT/Ja-1–1.1	0.000000	.0856	0.000	1,042	0.43	1,423.8	25.8	1,330	5	2.90	1.9	.2459	1.9	.990
VT/Ja-1–2.1	-0.000004	.0848	-0.007	1,180	0.38	1,430.9	26.2	1,312	10	2.89	2.0	.2470	1.9	.966
VT/Ja-1–3.1	-0.000008	.0852	-0.015	1,305	0.48	1,335.6	24.2	1,324	5	2.71	1.9	.2301	1.9	.989
VT/Ja-1–4.1	0.000000	.0856	-0.001	1,267	0.44	1,378.9	24.9	1,330	5	2.81	1.9	.2379	1.9	.991
VT/Ja-1–5.1	0.000000	.0838	0.000	1,505	0.40	1,402.7	25.4	1,289	8	2.79	1.9	.2416	1.9	.978
VT/Ja-1–6.1	0.000000	.0849	0.000	1,131	0.39	1,341.5	25.5	1,313	6	2.70	2.0	.2310	2.0	.987
VT/Ja-1–7.1	0.000000	.0853	0.000	1,204	0.42	1,340.4	24.3	1,321	5	2.71	1.9	.2309	1.9	.989
VT/Ja-1–8.1	0.000000	.0860	0.000	903	0.40	1,309.3	24.3	1,337	13	2.67	2.0	.2255	1.9	.947

Table 3. Sensitive high resolution ion microprobe (SHRIMP) uranium-thorium-lead (U-Th-Pb) data for zircon and monazite from rocks of Vermont.—Continued

[Abbreviations are as follows: Ma, millions of years (mega-annum); NA, not applicable; ppm, parts per million; —, measured ^{204}Pb below detection limit; ρ, error correlation]

Analysis[1]	Measured ^{204}Pb/^{206}Pb	Measured ^{207}Pb/^{206}Pb	Percent common ^{206}Pb	Uranium (ppm)	Th/U	^{206}Pb/^{238}U (Ma)[2]	Error (Ma)[3]	^{207}Pb/^{206}Pb (Ma)[2]	Error (Ma)[3]	^{207}Pb/^{235}U[4]	Error (percent)[3]	^{206}Pb/^{238}U[4]	Error (percent)[3]	ρ
VT/Ja-1-9.1	0.000001	.0855	0.002	1,329	0.45	1,358.4	24.8	1,329	5	2.76	1.9	.2342	1.9	.991
VT/Ja-1-10.1	0.000001	.0856	0.001	1,116	0.44	1,372.1	25.3	1,330	6	2.79	1.9	.2367	1.9	.988
VT/Ja-1-11.1	0.000000	.0855	0.000	1,210	0.46	1,344.7	24.3	1,328	5	2.73	1.9	.2318	1.9	.990
VT/Lu 1-91 (Fine-grained granodiorite of the Ludlow Mountain granodiorite gneiss at Okemo Mountain)														
VT/Lu-1-1.1	0.000016	.0854	0.03	190	0.43	1,259.7	11.0	1,320	12	2.54	1.1	.2165	0.9	.827
VT/Lu-1-2.1	0.000486	.1078	0.77	134	0.33	1,324.9	12.5	1,644	34	3.24	2.1	.2323	1.0	.475
VT/Lu-1-3.1	0.000035	.0850	0.06	215	0.39	1,233.1	13.3	1,305	13	2.47	1.3	.2116	1.1	.852
VT/Lu-1-4.1	0.000034	.0848	0.06	238	0.38	1,258.8	10.8	1,301	11	2.51	1.0	.2161	0.9	.855
VT/Lu-1-5.1	0.000021	.0854	0.03	299	0.42	1,297.3	11.0	1,318	9	2.62	1.0	.2231	0.9	.876
VT/Lu-1-6.1	-0.000009	.0801	-0.02	375	0.16	1,099.9	9.5	1,203	10	2.07	1.0	.1869	0.9	.875
VT/Lu-1-7.1	-0.000014	.0843	-0.02	271	0.31	1,251.6	10.8	1,305	10	2.50	1.0	.2149	0.9	.874
VT/Lu-1-8.1	0.000053	.0856	0.09	221	0.39	1,274.5	11.1	1,313	12	2.56	1.1	.2190	0.9	.819
VT/Lu-1-9.1	0.000131	.0852	0.22	206	0.33	1,158.7	10.2	1,277	17	2.28	1.3	.1980	0.9	.723
VT/Lu-1-10.1	-0.000004	.0850	-0.01	255	0.46	1,263.4	10.9	1,317	9	2.55	1.0	.2171	0.9	.882
VT/Lu-1-11.1	0.000029	.0854	0.05	399	0.40	1,291.5	10.8	1,316	8	2.60	1.0	.2221	0.9	.897
VT/Lu-1-12.1	0.000050	.0852	0.08	266	0.55	1,229.5	10.6	1,305	10	2.46	1.0	.2109	0.9	.859
VT/Lu-1-13.1	0.000094	.0871	0.16	141	0.43	1,198.9	11.1	1,334	19	2.43	1.4	.2058	1.0	.702
VT/Lu-1-14.1	-0.000061	.0854	-0.10	102	0.35	1,272.3	12.3	1,344	17	2.60	1.3	.2190	1.0	.746
VT/Lu-1-15.1	0.000061	.0854	0.10	269	0.40	1,246.3	10.7	1,306	12	2.49	1.1	.2139	0.9	.827
VT/Lu-1-16.1	0.000035	.0853	0.06	453	0.41	1,249.6	10.4	1,311	9	2.51	1.0	.2146	0.9	.881
VT/Lu-1-17.1	0.000039	.0854	0.06	280	0.48	1,250.7	11.6	1,313	11	2.51	1.1	.2148	1.0	.857
VT/Lu-1-18.1	-0.000027	.0861	-0.04	249	0.45	1,296.7	11.2	1,350	10	2.66	1.0	.2234	0.9	.869
VT/Lu-1-19.1	0.000044	.0808	0.07	1,265	0.23	1,247.5	10.1	1,202	6	2.36	0.9	.2130	0.8	.939
VT/Lu-1-20.1	0.000013	.0843	0.02	695	0.35	1,343.9	11.0	1,294	7	2.68	0.9	.2312	0.8	.927
VT/Lu 2-91 (Okemo Quartzite–Detrital zircon)														
VT/Lu-2-1	—	.0855	0.00	213	0.48	1,181.8	12.4	1,327	22	2.39	1.6	.2027	1.1	.692
VT/Lu-2-2	—	.0875	0.00	196	0.48	1,163.9	12.4	1,371	24	2.41	1.6	.1999	1.1	.668
VT/Lu-2-3	—	.0864	0.00	113	0.78	1,239.8	13.9	1,348	29	2.54	1.9	.2132	1.2	.613
VT/Lu-2-4	—	.0867	0.00	206	0.40	1,265.4	13.3	1,353	21	2.60	1.5	.2179	1.1	.706
VT/Lu-2-5	—	.0869	0.00	351	0.48	1,270.4	13.0	1,359	16	2.62	1.4	.2188	1.1	.783
VT/Lu-2-6	—	.0875	0.00	99	0.56	1,211.2	14.2	1,371	33	2.51	2.1	.2084	1.2	.577
VT/Lu-2-7	0.000049	.0852	0.08	205	0.58	1,364.8	14.4	1,303	22	2.74	1.6	.2350	1.1	.686
VT/Lu-2-8	0.000043	.0867	0.07	283	0.42	1,286.9	13.2	1,341	19	2.63	1.5	.2216	1.1	.725
VT/Lu-2-9	0.000076	.0832	0.13	111	0.51	1,143.0	13.1	1,249	48	2.21	2.7	.1950	1.2	.429

Table 3. Sensitive high resolution ion microprobe (SHRIMP) uranium-thorium-lead (U-Th-Pb) data for zircon and monazite from rocks of Vermont.—Continued

[Abbreviations are as follows: Ma, millions of years (mega-annum); NA, not applicable; ppm, parts per million; —, measured ^{204}Pb below detection limit; ρ, error correlation]

Analysis[1]	Measured ^{204}Pb/^{206}Pb	Measured ^{207}Pb/^{206}Pb	Percent common ^{206}Pb	Uranium (ppm)	Th/U	^{206}Pb/^{238}U (Ma)[2]	Error (Ma)[3]	^{207}Pb/^{206}Pb (Ma)[2]	Error (Ma)[3]	^{207}Pb/^{235}U[4]	Error (percent)[3]	^{206}Pb/^{238}U[4]	Error (percent)[3]	ρ
VT/Lu 2–91(Okemo Quartzite–Detrital zircon)—Continued														
VT/Lu-2-10	—	.0798	0.00	340	0.19	964.1	10.3	1,192	26	1.79	1.7	.1630	1.1	.647
VT/Lu-2-11	—	.0863	0.00	239	0.38	1,336.0	13.8	1,344	19	2.74	1.5	.2304	1.1	.733
VT/Lu-2-12	—	.0854	0.00	137	0.83	1,338.3	14.6	1,324	26	2.71	1.7	.2306	1.1	.647
VT/Lu-2-13	0.000119	.0843	0.20	154	0.29	1,284.2	14.0	1,261	31	2.51	1.9	.2202	1.1	.579
VT/Lu-2-14	—	.0855	0.00	296	0.21	1,386.5	14.4	1,328	19	2.82	1.5	.2392	1.1	.734
VT/Lu-2-15	—	.0839	0.00	91	0.69	1,333.9	15.4	1,291	31	2.65	2.0	.2294	1.2	.594
VT/Lu-2-16	0.000046	.0857	0.08	94	0.54	1,366.7	15.7	1,318	31	2.76	2.0	.2356	1.2	.588
MC6000 (Megacrystic augen gneiss at Brandon Gap)														
MC6000-1.1	0.000115	.0795	0.19	229	0.69	1,130.7	14.0	1,144	24	2.06	1.8	.1918	1.3	.723
MC6000-2.1	0.000141	.0791	0.24	150	0.49	1,134.7	12.2	1,124	31	2.05	1.9	.1924	1.1	.588
MC6000-2.2	0.000060	.0735	0.10	753	0.00	1,093.7	9.5	1,003	11	1.84	1.0	.1842	0.9	.868
MC6000-3.1	0.000682	.0796	1.17	29	0.48	1,162.1	20.8	924	146	1.88	7.4	.1955	1.9	.261
MC6000-4.1	0.000518	.0816	0.88	30	0.43	1,136.1	21.1	1,047	99	1.96	5.3	.1919	2.0	.370
MC6000-5.1	0.000217	.0791	0.37	123	0.47	1,173.2	13.3	1,096	40	2.08	2.3	.1989	1.2	.511
MC6000-6.1	0.000107	.0774	0.18	98	0.49	1,172.7	13.9	1,092	44	2.08	2.5	.1988	1.2	.489
MC6000-6.2	0.000127	.0791	0.21	178	0.25	1,133.1	15.4	1,129	26	2.05	1.9	.1921	1.4	.728
MC6000-7.1	0.000109	.0808	0.18	81	0.50	1,146.9	15.0	1,178	35	2.13	2.2	.1950	1.4	.611
MC6000-8.1	0.000132	.0802	0.22	194	0.32	1,161.7	12.2	1,154	25	2.13	1.7	.1974	1.1	.652
MC6000-9.1	-0.000054	.0791	-0.09	152	0.51	1,184.6	13.1	1,194	20	2.22	1.5	.2018	1.1	.746
MC6000-10.1	0.000203	.0784	0.34	137	0.49	1,138.4	12.9	1,082	37	2.01	2.2	.1926	1.2	.544
MC6000-11.1	0.000136	.0789	0.23	144	0.31	1,132.8	12.9	1,121	33	2.04	2.0	.1920	1.2	.584
MC6000-12.1	0.000096	.0786	0.16	171	0.41	1,169.9	12.8	1,128	29	2.12	1.9	.1986	1.1	.614
MC6000-13.1	-0.000019	.0790	-0.03	224	0.50	1,158.2	15.0	1,180	16	2.15	1.6	.1970	1.3	.850
MC6000-14.1	0.000096	.0789	0.16	127	0.62	1,155.1	15.7	1,136	29	2.10	2.0	.1961	1.4	.695
MC6000-14.2	0.000112	.0782	0.19	187	0.25	1,176.2	12.4	1,111	28	2.11	1.8	.1996	1.1	.615
MC6000-15.1	0.000033	.0789	0.05	654	0.24	1,194.0	10.7	1,157	10	2.20	1.1	.2031	0.9	.872
R2008 (Migmatite gneiss in Pine Hill slice)														
R2008-1.1	-0.000003	.0732	-0.22	592	0.45	1,070.8	19.9	1,022	12	1.82	2.0	.1803	1.9	.956
R2008-2.1	-0.000015	.0735	-0.11	584	0.34	1,053.9	19.6	1,034	12	1.80	2.0	.1775	1.9	.953
R2008-3.1	0.000042	.0738	-0.01	573	0.26	1,038.7	19.4	1,019	19	1.76	2.1	.1747	1.9	.903
R2008-4.1	-0.000020	.0730	-0.11	407	0.30	1,040.4	19.6	1,023	15	1.77	2.1	.1750	2.0	.937
R2008-5.1	-0.000006	.0731	-0.19	610	0.34	1,059.8	19.7	1,018	12	1.80	2.0	.1784	1.9	.954
R2008-6.1	0.000042	.0737	-0.01	480	0.27	1,036.3	19.4	1,017	17	1.76	2.1	.1743	1.9	.919
R2008-7.1	0.000023	.0750	0.09	444	0.21	1,046.7	19.6	1,059	17	1.81	2.1	.1764	1.9	.918

13

Table 3. Sensitive high resolution ion microprobe (SHRIMP) uranium-thorium-lead (U-Th-Pb) data for zircon and monazite from rocks of Vermont.—Continued

[Abbreviations are as follows: Ma, millions of years (mega-annum); NA, not applicable; ppm, parts per million; —, measured ^{204}Pb below detection limit; ρ, error correlation]

Analysis[1]	Measured ^{204}Pb/^{206}Pb	Measured ^{207}Pb/^{206}Pb	Percent common ^{206}Pb	Uranium (ppm)	Th/U	^{206}Pb/^{238}U (Ma)[2]	Error (Ma)[3]	^{207}Pb/^{206}Pb (Ma)[2]	Error (Ma)[3]	^{207}Pb/^{235}U[4]	Error (percent)[3]	^{206}Pb/^{238}U[4]	Error (percent)[3]	ρ
						R2008 (Migmatite gneiss in Pine Hill slice)—Continued								
R2008-8.1	-0.000033	.0745	0.47	452	0.16	945.0	17.7	1,066	16	1.64	2.1	.1587	1.9	.924
R2008-8.2	0.000021	.0743	0.03	582	0.47	1,042.8	19.4	1,042	15	1.79	2.1	.1756	1.9	.930
R2008-9.1	0.000018	.0737	-0.07	667	0.35	1,050.1	19.5	1,026	12	1.79	2.0	.1767	1.9	.955
R2008-10.1	-0.000086	.0721	-0.26	383	0.20	1,047.6	19.6	1,022	22	1.78	2.2	.1763	1.9	.877
R2008-10.2	-0.000059	.0744	-0.04	423	0.29	1,061.3	22.7	1,075	27	1.86	2.6	.1791	2.2	.858
R2008-11.1	-0.000101	.0739	0.27	424	0.18	976.2	19.4	1,079	23	1.71	2.3	.1642	2.1	.876
R2008R-1.1	-0.000003	.0743	0.18	1,138	0.13	1,006.8	19.5	1,049	11	1.73	2.1	.1693	2.0	.967
R2008R-1.2	—	.0739	0.02	1,019	0.08	1,033.9	19.1	1,039	9	1.77	2.0	.1740	1.9	.972
R2008R-2.1	0.000029	.0737	-0.02	596	0.46	1,037.3	19.3	1,022	13	1.76	2.0	.1745	1.9	.947
R2008R-3.1	0.000038	.0744	0.06	541	0.34	1,038.9	19.8	1,038	15	1.78	2.1	.1749	2.0	.936
R2008R-3.2	0.000028	.0744	0.06	683	0.41	1,037.1	19.7	1,040	12	1.78	2.1	.1746	2.0	.957
R2008R-3.3	0.000029	.0750	0.07	396	0.30	1,051.5	52.4	1,057	38	1.82	5.5	.1772	5.2	.939
						VT/Br 2-89 (Newfane tonalite intruding Cram Hill Formation near South Newfane)								
VT/Br-2-1.1	0.000075	.0572	-0.15	100	0.71	543.7	8.1	NA	NA	0.68	2.4	.0878	1.5	.643
VT/Br-2-2.1	0.000077	.0561	-0.23	154	0.73	530.9	7.8	NA	NA	0.65	2.2	.0855	1.5	.680
VT/Br-2-3.1	—	.0588	0.08	141	0.72	534.4	8.0	NA	NA	0.70	2.2	.0865	1.5	.697
VT/Br-2-4.1	0.000040	.0574	0.01	207	0.82	505.2	7.4	NA	NA	0.64	2.1	.0815	1.5	.716
VT/Br-2-5.1	0.000038	.0588	0.17	314	0.88	507.1	7.3	NA	NA	0.66	1.9	.0819	1.5	.768
VT/Br-2-6.1	0.000213	.0547	-0.34	181	0.57	506.9	7.5	NA	NA	0.58	4.3	.0812	1.5	.354
VT/Br-2-7.1	0.000069	.0567	-0.08	302	0.66	504.2	7.2	NA	NA	0.62	2.2	.0812	1.5	.676
VT/Br-2-8.1	0.000017	.0914	-0.36	153	0.52	1,518.9	21.7	NA	NA	3.33	1.6	.2647	1.5	.898
VT/Br-2-9.1	—	.0573	-0.02	266	0.73	510.4	7.3	NA	NA	0.65	1.8	.0824	1.5	.793
VT/Br-2-10.1	—	.0566	-0.06	76	0.57	495.8	8.3	NA	NA	0.62	2.9	.0799	1.7	.594
VT/Br-2-11.1	—	.0561	-0.13	173	0.51	495.1	7.4	NA	NA	0.62	2.4	.0797	1.5	.642
VT/Br-2-12.1	0.000149	.0619	0.06	147	1.68	652.9	9.7	NA	NA	0.88	2.6	.1064	1.5	.588
VT/Br-2-13.1	0.000056	.0555	-0.22	178	0.62	504.4	7.5	NA	NA	0.61	2.3	.0811	1.5	.663
VT/Br-2-14.1	—	.0568	-0.04	218	0.69	497.1	7.3	NA	NA	0.63	2.1	.0801	1.5	.726
VT/Br-2-15.1	—	.0560	-0.15	82	0.64	501.0	9.3	NA	NA	0.62	3.0	.0807	1.9	.634
VT/Br-2-16.1	0.000384	.0559	-0.24	83	0.55	524.2	8.5	NA	NA	0.58	5.8	.0839	1.7	.285
VT/Br-2-17.1	0.000107	.0558	-0.19	195	0.37	505.7	7.5	NA	NA	0.61	2.7	.0813	1.5	.559
VT/Br-2-18.1	0.000044	.0562	-0.12	547	0.76	499.5	7.1	NA	NA	0.62	1.9	.0804	1.4	.779
VT/Br-2-19.1	—	.0573	0.01	287	0.86	499.3	7.3	NA	NA	0.64	2.0	.0805	1.5	.754

14

Table 3. Sensitive high resolution ion microprobe (SHRIMP) uranium-thorium-lead (U-Th-Pb) data for zircon and monazite from rocks of Vermont.—Continued

[Abbreviations are as follows: Ma, millions of years (mega-annum); NA, not applicable; ppm, parts per million; —, measured [204]Pb below detection limit; ρ, error correlation]

Analysis[1]	Measured [204]Pb/[206]Pb	Measured [207]Pb/[206]Pb	Percent common [206]Pb	Uranium (ppm)	Th/U	[206]Pb/[238]U (Ma)[2]	Error (Ma)[3]	[207]Pb/[206]Pb (Ma)[2]	Error (Ma)[3]	[207]Pb/[235]U	Error (percent)[3]	[206]Pb/[238]U[4]	Error (percent)[3]	ρ
VT/Br 2-89 (Newfane tonalite intruding Cram Hill Formation near South Newfane)—Continued															
VT/Br-2-20.1	0.000139	.0575	0.02	82	0.60	504.4	10.0	NA	NA	0.62	3.7	.0812	2.0	.542
VT/Br-2-21.1	—	.0555	-0.25	229	0.58	512.5	7.5	NA	NA	0.63	2.1	.0825	1.5	.725
VT/Br-2-7.2	0.000200	.0590	0.18	167	0.61	511.8	7.7	NA	NA	0.64	3.1	.0825	1.5	.489
L-18 (Trondhjemite in Barnard Gneiss proper (of Richardson, 1924) north of Proctorsville)															
L18-3.1	0.000013	.0571	0.00	1,580	1.22	494.3	7.1	NA	NA	0.63	1.6	.0797	1.5	.925
L18-4.1	0.000175	.0570	-0.03	285	0.99	497.8	7.6	NA	NA	0.60	2.6	.0800	1.6	.601
L18-5.1	0.000030	.0579	0.05	744	0.73	510.2	7.4	NA	NA	0.65	1.8	.0824	1.5	.849
L18-6.1	0.000054	.0827	0.01	158	0.48	1,258.6	19.3	NA	NA	2.43	1.9	.2154	1.6	.815
L18-7.1	-0.000017	.0575	0.09	163	0.48	484.6	8.5	NA	NA	0.62	2.6	.0782	1.8	.697
L18-8.1	0.001953	.0755	2.15	110	0.55	528.8	12.2	NA	NA	0.54	15.8	.0843	2.4	.152
L18-9.1	0.000238	.0563	-0.11	278	0.83	498.5	8.5	NA	NA	0.58	3.5	.0800	1.8	.504
L18-10.1	0.000101	.0570	-0.01	339	0.62	494.5	7.6	NA	NA	0.61	2.3	.0796	1.6	.674
L18-11.1	-0.000015	.0573	-0.02	920	0.48	508.6	7.4	NA	NA	0.65	1.6	.0821	1.5	.902
SP450 (Felsic volcanic layer within Cram Hill Formation at Springfield)															
SP450-1.1	-0.000101	.0568	-0.18	345	1.05	490.2	6.2	NA	NA	0.64	2.2	.0791	1.3	.596
SP450-2.1	0.000204	.0573	0.37	187	0.54	481.4	6.7	NA	NA	0.58	3.1	.0773	1.4	.465
SP450-3.1	0.000182	.0593	0.33	85	0.36	477.1	7.9	NA	NA	0.60	5.8	.0768	1.7	.294
SP450-4.1	-0.000084	.0577	-0.15	197	0.40	487.2	6.7	NA	NA	0.64	2.4	.0787	1.4	.592
SP450-5.1	0.000084	.0575	0.15	211	0.42	481.8	6.6	NA	NA	0.60	3.0	.0776	1.4	.466
SP450-6.1	-0.000058	.0571	-0.10	137	0.43	475.1	7.1	NA	NA	0.61	2.6	.0766	1.5	.592
SP450-7.1	0.000006	.0571	0.01	414	0.51	491.1	6.1	NA	NA	0.62	1.7	.0792	1.3	.761
SP450-8.1	0.000074	.0590	0.13	151	0.49	478.5	7.0	NA	NA	0.62	3.0	.0772	1.5	.497
SP450-9.1	-0.000077	.0572	-0.14	149	0.52	482.3	7.0	NA	NA	0.63	3.0	.0778	1.5	.498
SP450-10.1	0.000031	.0554	0.05	291	0.74	488.7	6.6	NA	NA	0.60	2.2	.0786	1.4	.630
SP450-11.1	0.000000	.0565	0.00	674	0.89	485.4	5.8	NA	NA	0.61	1.5	.0782	1.2	.825
SP450-12.1	-0.000544	.0584	-0.98	79	0.37	476.3	8.4	NA	NA	0.71	5.9	.0776	1.8	.308
SP450-13.1	0.000021	.0583	0.04	235	0.46	489.3	6.4	NA	NA	0.63	1.9	.0790	1.3	.685
SP450-14.1	-0.000170	.0595	-0.30	75	0.39	475.7	7.7	NA	NA	0.66	3.5	.0771	1.7	.472
SP450-15.1	0.000119	.0571	0.21	126	0.69	476.0	6.9	NA	NA	0.58	3.2	.0765	1.5	.463
SP450-16.1	0.000019	.0583	0.03	223	0.44	482.5	6.4	NA	NA	0.62	2.1	.0778	1.4	.653
SP450-17.1	-0.000149	.0575	-0.27	142	0.42	468.2	6.7	NA	NA	0.62	4.4	.0756	1.5	.339
SP450-18.1	0.000080	.0574	0.14	257	0.62	477.4	6.2	NA	NA	0.60	2.7	.0768	1.3	.497
SP450-19.1	-0.000002	.0564	0.00	249	0.43	475.5	6.2	NA	NA	0.59	1.9	.0765	1.3	.695
SP450-20.1	0.000045	.0562	0.08	286	0.54	487.5	6.2	NA	NA	0.60	2.2	.0784	1.3	.580

Table 3. Sensitive high resolution ion microprobe (SHRIMP) uranium-thorium-lead (U-Th-Pb) data for zircon and monazite from rocks of Vermont.—Continued

[Abbreviations are as follows: Ma, millions of years (mega-annum); ppm, parts per million; —, measured ^{204}Pb below detection limit; NA, not applicable; ρ, error correlation]

Analysis[1]	Measured ^{204}Pb/^{206}Pb	Measured ^{207}Pb/^{206}Pb	Percent common ^{206}Pb	Uranium (ppm)	Th/U	^{206}Pb/^{238}U (Ma)[2]	Error (Ma)[3]	^{207}Pb/^{206}Pb (Ma)[2]	Error (Ma)[3]	^{207}Pb/^{235}U[4]	Error (percent)[3]	^{206}Pb/^{238}U[4]	Error (percent)[3]	ρ
MC3432 (Granite in the Braintree Intrusive Complex)														
MC3432–1	0.000328	.0532	-0.21	136	0.65	407.9	8.5	NA	NA	0.43	5.8	.0648	2.1	.372
MC3432–2	—	.0582	0.43	153	0.38	401.9	8.4	NA	NA	0.52	3.7	.0646	2.1	.575
MC3432–3	0.000125	.0569	0.21	267	0.52	420.8	8.4	NA	NA	0.51	3.4	.0674	2.0	.593
MC3432–4	—	.0566	0.19	444	0.83	417.0	8.1	NA	NA	0.52	2.7	.0670	2.0	.741
MC3432–5	—	.0560	0.06	234	0.53	432.5	8.7	NA	NA	0.54	3.1	.0694	2.0	.661
MC3432–6	—	.0551	0.05	674	0.37	402.1	7.8	NA	NA	0.49	2.5	.0644	2.0	.785
MC3432–7	—	.0545	-0.11	239	0.49	430.5	9.2	NA	NA	0.52	3.2	.0690	2.2	.680
MC3432–8	0.000405	.0599	0.57	192	0.77	426.1	8.7	NA	NA	0.51	5.2	.0682	2.1	.400
MC3432–9	0.000176	.0579	0.35	602	0.43	413.6	8.0	NA	NA	0.51	2.9	.0663	2.0	.676
MC3432–10	—	.0545	-0.04	148	0.83	406.8	8.5	NA	NA	0.49	3.7	.0651	2.1	.579
MC3432–11	0.000148	.0557	0.00	371	0.52	438.5	8.6	NA	NA	0.52	3.3	.0702	2.0	.614
MC3432–12	0.000087	.0542	-0.18	397	0.48	437.0	8.6	NA	NA	0.51	3.1	.0699	2.0	.660
MC3432–13	—	.0582	0.39	234	0.51	413.6	8.4	NA	NA	0.53	3.2	.0665	2.1	.650
MC3432–14	—	.0554	0.02	392	0.50	420.9	8.3	NA	NA	0.52	2.7	.0675	2.0	.732
MC3432–15	—	.0586	0.45	257	0.42	411.2	8.2	NA	NA	0.53	3.0	.0662	2.0	.677
MC3432–16	0.000126	.0548	-0.09	317	0.56	433.4	8.5	NA	NA	0.51	3.2	.0693	2.0	.618
VT–Nq–1–97 (Trondhjemite of the Newport Intrusive Complex)														
VT–Nq–1–1.1	—	.0563	0.12	1,105	0.37	425.2	3.3	NA	NA	0.53	1.2	.0683	0.8	.637
VT–Nq–1–2.1	0.000018	.0543	-0.04	636	0.46	395.8	3.3	NA	NA	0.47	1.6	.0633	0.8	.533
VT–Nq–1–3.1	0.000015	.0552	-0.02	980	0.25	428.0	3.4	NA	NA	0.52	1.3	.0686	0.8	.615
VT–Nq–1–4.1	0.000016	.0552	0.02	1,177	0.35	414.0	3.3	NA	NA	0.50	1.3	.0663	0.8	.610
VT–Nq–1–5.1	0.000255	.0593	0.63	1,010	0.52	378.9	3.1	NA	NA	0.46	2.1	.0606	0.8	.393
VT–Nq–1–6.1	-0.000019	.0550	-0.05	768	0.34	427.1	3.4	NA	NA	0.52	1.4	.0685	0.8	.598
VT–Nq–1–7.1	0.000040	.0555	0.04	700	0.29	422.7	3.5	NA	NA	0.51	1.6	.0677	0.8	.538
VT–Nq–1–8.1	0.000044	.0554	0.01	986	0.35	425.9	3.4	NA	NA	0.52	1.4	.0682	0.8	.571
VT–Nq–1–9.1	—	.0562	0.17	1,142	0.32	403.9	3.2	NA	NA	0.50	1.3	.0648	0.8	.612
VT–Nq–1–10.1	0.000697	.0636	1.10	1,718	0.71	399.5	3.1	NA	NA	0.47	3.6	.0638	0.8	.220
VT–Nq–1–11.1	0.000148	.0571	0.23	1,105	0.46	422.3	3.3	NA	NA	0.51	1.6	.0677	0.8	.510
VT–Nq–1–12.1	0.000863	.0672	1.61	876	1.13	379.0	3.1	NA	NA	0.46	3.8	.0606	0.8	.220
VT–Nq–1–13.1	0.000020	.0563	0.12	1,008	0.42	424.1	3.3	NA	NA	0.53	1.3	.0681	0.8	.619
VT–Nq–1–14.1	0.000006	.0559	-0.03	2,852	0.23	457.8	3.3	NA	NA	0.57	0.9	.0736	0.7	.807
VT–CSTR–2 (Granite in Chester dome)														
VT–CSTR–2–1.1	0.000114	.0561	0.06	524	0.06	438.4	4.9	NA	NA	0.53	2.2	.0703	1.1	.532
VT–CSTR–2–2.1	0.000075	.0885	0.05	230	0.39	1,385.6	17.3	NA	NA	2.89	1.6	.2396	1.3	.791
VT–CSTR–2–3.1	0.000022	.0546	-0.01	2,130	0.07	398.6	4.9	NA	NA	0.48	1.5	.0637	1.3	.858

16

Table 3. Sensitive high resolution ion microprobe (SHRIMP) uranium-thorium-lead (U-Th-Pb) data for zircon and monazite from rocks of Vermont.—Continued

[Abbreviations are as follows: Ma, millions of years (mega-annum); NA, not applicable; ppm, parts per million; —, measured ^{204}Pb below detection limit; ρ, error correlation]

Analysis[1]	Measured ^{204}Pb/^{206}Pb	Measured ^{207}Pb/^{206}Pb	Percent common ^{206}Pb	Uranium (ppm)	Th/U	^{206}Pb/^{238}U (Ma)[2]	Error (Ma)[3]	^{207}Pb/^{206}Pb (Ma)[2]	Error (Ma)[3]	^{207}Pb/^{235}U[4]	Error (percent)[3]	^{206}Pb/^{238}U[4]	Error (percent)[3]	ρ
						VT–CSTR–2 (Granite in Chester dome)—Continued								
VT–CSTR–2–4.1	0.000272	.0579	0.41	141	0.04	395.9	5.7	NA	NA	0.47	5.5	.0633	1.5	.270
VT–CSTR–2–4.2	0.000731	.0628	1.01	40	0.01	394.5	8.3	NA	NA	0.45	13.4	.0629	2.2	.164
VT–CSTR–2–3.2	—	.0787	0.07	147	0.47	1,149.8	14.3	NA	NA	2.12	1.9	.1954	1.3	.662
VT–CSTR–2–5.1	0.000114	.0580	0.43	604	0.01	390.7	4.4	NA	NA	0.49	2.2	.0626	1.1	.513
VT–CSTR–2–6.1	0.000051	.0539	-0.05	795	0.04	384.8	4.2	NA	NA	0.45	1.9	.0614	1.1	.597
VT–CSTR–2–7.1	0.000030	.0543	-0.09	1,417	0.10	411.2	4.4	NA	NA	0.49	1.6	.0658	1.1	.697
VT–CSTR–2–8.1	—	.0564	0.27	886	0.07	380.0	4.2	NA	NA	0.47	2.3	.0609	1.1	.486
VT–CSTR–2–9.1	—	.0543	-0.01	1,623	0.09	387.9	4.1	NA	NA	0.46	1.4	.0620	1.1	.767
VT–CSTR–2–10.1	0.000012	.0546	-0.04	2,552	0.06	406.9	4.3	NA	NA	0.49	1.3	.0651	1.1	.815
VT–CSTR–2–10.1	—	.0837	0.06	136	0.39	1,274.0	16.1	NA	NA	2.52	1.9	.2187	1.3	.686
VT–CSTR–2–11.1	0.000033	.0557	0.09	1,409	0.07	412.5	4.7	NA	NA	0.50	1.9	.0661	1.2	.610
VT–CSTR–2–12.1	—	.0551	0.08	1,634	0.12	390.6	6.4	NA	NA	0.47	1.9	.0625	1.7	.878
VT–CSTR–2–13.1	0.000031	.0539	-0.08	2,743	0.08	393.3	4.4	NA	NA	0.46	1.4	.0628	1.1	.784
VT–CSTR–2–14.1	0.000035	.0552	0.08	2,124	0.04	394.2	4.2	NA	NA	0.48	1.4	.0631	1.1	.778
VT–CSTR–2–15.1	0.000015	.0541	-0.02	2,012	0.14	384.7	4.8	NA	NA	0.46	1.8	.0615	1.3	.715
						Barre#2 (Barre Granite)								
BARRE–1.1	—	.0537	-0.16	18,759	0.36	414.0	5.3	NA	NA	0.49	1.3	.0662	1.3	.976
BARRE–2.1	—	.0550	0.15	811	0.14	362.0	5.7	NA	NA	0.44	2.1	.0578	1.6	.756
BARRE–3.1	0.000255	.0570	0.39	1,170	0.12	365.5	5.1	NA	NA	0.43	2.5	.0583	1.4	.571
BARRE–4.1	0.000027	.0547	0.10	1,023	0.13	366.2	4.7	NA	NA	0.44	1.8	.0585	1.3	.713
BARRE–5.1	0.000133	.0565	0.34	1,317	0.18	363.7	6.0	NA	NA	0.44	2.2	.0581	1.7	.751
BARRE–6.1	0.000016	.0541	0.02	1,893	0.24	369.6	4.7	NA	NA	0.44	1.6	.0590	1.3	.798
BARRE–7.1	0.000029	.0544	0.05	1,595	0.25	372.0	5.3	NA	NA	0.44	2.0	.0594	1.4	.742
BARRE–8.1	—	.0544	0.04	2,177	0.37	376.8	5.1	NA	NA	0.45	1.6	.0602	1.4	.853
BARRE–9.1	—	.0536	-0.05	1,191	0.15	368.9	4.9	NA	NA	0.43	1.9	.0589	1.4	.726
BARRE–10.1	0.000036	.0560	0.22	910	0.21	379.2	4.9	NA	NA	0.46	1.9	.0607	1.3	.696
BARRE–11.1	0.000021	.0551	0.17	1,630	0.21	360.4	4.6	NA	NA	0.43	1.6	.0576	1.3	.803
BARRE–12.1	0.000012	.0535	-0.06	1,480	0.24	370.4	4.9	NA	NA	0.43	1.7	.0591	1.3	.796
BARRE–13.1	0.000038	.0527	-0.14	1,260	0.17	365.5	4.7	NA	NA	0.42	1.8	.0582	1.3	.714
BARRE–14.1	—	.0553	0.15	2,060	0.29	374.1	4.8	NA	NA	0.46	1.6	.0598	1.3	.831
BARRE–15.1	0.000042	.0544	0.06	935	0.14	367.9	4.8	NA	NA	0.44	1.9	.0587	1.3	.698
						VT/Br 1–89 (Black Mountain pluton)								
VT/Br1–1.1	—	.0526	-0.10	560	0.30	345.0	5.0	NA	NA	0.40	2.4	.0549	1.5	.612
VT/Br1–2.1	—	.0539	0.08	644	0.25	342.5	4.6	NA	NA	0.41	3.1	.0546	1.4	.446

Table 3. Sensitive high resolution ion microprobe (SHRIMP) uranium-thorium-lead (U-Th-Pb) data for zircon and monazite from rocks of Vermont.—Continued

[Abbreviations are as follows: Ma, millions of years (mega-annum); NA, not applicable; ppm, parts per million; —, measured [204]Pb below detection limit; ρ, error correlation]

Analysis[1]	Measured [204]Pb/[206]Pb	Measured [207]Pb/[206]Pb	Percent common [206]Pb	Uranium (ppm)	Th/U	[206]Pb/[238]U (Ma)[2]	Error (Ma)[3]	[207]Pb/[206]Pb (Ma)[2]	Error (Ma)[3]	[207]Pb/[235]U[4]	Error (percent)[3]	[206]Pb/[238]U[4]	Error (percent)[3]	ρ
				VT/Br 1–89 (Black Mountain pluton)—Continued										
VT/Br1–3.1	0.000059	.0533	0.03	452	0.24	331.3	8.1	NA	NA	0.38	3.3	.0527	2.5	.748
VT/Br1–4.1	—	.0551	0.20	682	0.25	350.4	6.7	NA	NA	0.43	2.5	.0560	1.9	.769
VT/Br1–5.1	0.000128	.0532	-0.06	367	0.31	355.2	6.7	NA	NA	0.40	3.4	.0565	1.9	.567
VT/Br1–5.2	0.000044	.0548	-0.10	28,188	0.02	434.4	5.4	NA	NA	0.52	1.3	.0696	1.3	.974
VT/Br1–6.1	0.000102	.0554	0.10	233	0.27	395.5	7.4	NA	NA	0.47	3.5	.0632	1.9	.546
VT/Br1–7.1	—	.0506	-0.42	276	0.14	371.1	7.5	NA	NA	0.41	3.1	.0590	2.0	.661
VT/Br1–8.1	—	.0520	-0.24	560	0.34	369.2	6.8	NA	NA	0.42	2.5	.0588	1.9	.752
VT/Br1–9.1	—	.0533	-0.07	309	0.29	364.7	8.1	NA	NA	0.43	3.1	.0582	2.3	.721
VT/Br1–10.1	—	.0540	0.05	478	0.36	353.0	5.8	NA	NA	0.42	2.4	.0563	1.7	.688
VT/Br1–11.1	—	.0554	0.18	448	0.34	370.0	5.0	NA	NA	0.45	2.2	.0592	1.4	.607
VT/Br1–12.1	0.000135	.0539	0.00	241	0.26	365.8	5.4	NA	NA	0.42	3.9	.0582	1.5	.382
VT/Br1–13.1	—	.0547	0.05	293	0.31	380.1	6.6	NA	NA	0.46	3.0	.0608	1.7	.584
VT/Br1–14.1	0.000045	.0538	0.08	516	0.37	335.0	4.6	NA	NA	0.39	2.4	.0533	1.4	.571
VT/Br1–15.1	0.000034	.0541	0.04	912	0.22	360.1	5.1	NA	NA	0.42	2.0	.0574	1.4	.715
VT/Br1–16.1	—	.0533	-0.06	479	0.19	361.1	8.7	NA	NA	0.42	3.0	.0576	2.4	.799
VT/Br1–17.1	0.000112	.0516	-0.16	488	0.29	325.8	6.2	NA	NA	0.36	3.0	.0517	1.9	.637
VT/Br1–18.1	—	.0534	-0.02	483	0.19	351.7	4.7	NA	NA	0.41	2.2	.0561	1.4	.608
VT/Br1–19.1	—	.0544	0.08	324	0.15	360.3	12.3	NA	NA	0.43	4.1	.0575	3.5	.850
VT/Br1–20.1	0.000436	.0586	0.59	863	0.20	363.2	8.2	NA	NA	0.42	4.8	.0578	2.3	.484
VT/Br1–21.1	0.000100	.0552	-0.09	19,799	0.03	447.0	5.6	NA	NA	0.53	1.3	.0716	1.3	.952
VT/Br1–22.1	0.000056	.0547	0.04	10,177	0.07	387.5	4.9	NA	NA	0.46	1.4	.0619	1.3	.907
VT/Br1–23.1	0.000100	.0551	0.11	20,856	0.02	378.9	4.8	NA	NA	0.45	1.3	.0605	1.3	.952
VT/Br1–24.1	0.000245	.0574	0.10	30,266	0.02	476.7	6.0	NA	NA	0.57	1.3	.0765	1.3	.952
VT/Br1–25.1	0.000033	.0544	-0.02	9,736	0.16	393.3	5.0	NA	NA	0.47	1.5	.0629	1.3	.831
mVT/Br11.2	0.000351	0.058	0.53	1,241	41.4	361.1	3.5	NA	NA	0.42	4.4	.0576	1.0	.227
mVT/Br113.2	0.000233	0.054	0.02	1,298	32.1	364.9	3.5	NA	NA	0.40	3.5	.0580	1.0	.277
mVT/Br13.1	0.000335	0.060	0.76	1,153	75.0	362.0	3.6	NA	NA	0.44	4.2	.0578	1.0	.240
mVT/Br14.1	0.000105	0.057	0.39	1,533	40.5	359.3	3.2	NA	NA	0.44	2.3	.0574	0.9	.399
mVT/Br114.1	0.000511	0.058	0.52	496	77.8	364.7	4.3	NA	NA	0.40	7.2	.0580	1.2	.173
mVT/Br114.2	0.000125	0.056	0.30	1,042	34.2	364.5	3.6	NA	NA	0.44	2.9	.0582	1.0	.340
mVT/Br15.1	0.000116	0.060	0.79	758	93.1	359.7	3.9	NA	NA	0.47	3.1	.0577	1.1	.345
mVT/Br15.2	0.000206	0.056	0.24	1,823	30.2	354.3	3.2	NA	NA	0.41	3.1	.0564	0.9	.300
mVT/Br115.1	0.000245	0.057	0.41	804	93.4	361.3	3.9	NA	NA	0.43	4.3	.0576	1.1	.257
mVT/Br16.1	0.000192	0.055	0.08	617	33.0	367.4	3.9	NA	NA	0.42	4.0	.0585	1.1	.272

Table 3. Sensitive high resolution ion microprobe (SHRIMP) uranium-thorium-lead (U-Th-Pb) data for zircon and monazite from rocks of Vermont.—Continued

[Abbreviations are as follows: Ma, millions of years (mega-annum); ppm, parts per million; —, measured 204Pb below detection limit; NA, not applicable; ρ, error correlation]

Analysis[1]	Measured 207Pb/206Pb	Measured 204Pb/206Pb	Percent common 206Pb	Uranium (ppm)	Th/U	206Pb/238U (Ma)[2]	Error (Ma)[3]	207Pb/206Pb (Ma)[2]	Error (Ma)[3]	207Pb/235U[4]	Error (percent)[3]	206Pb/238U[4]	Error (percent)[3]	ρ
						VT/Br 1–89 [Black Mountain pluton]—Continued								
mVT/Br117.1	0.000856	0.066	1.50	1,649	29.7	355.6	3.3	NA	NA	0.42	6.4	.0567	1.0	.150
mVT/Br117.2	0.000159	0.056	0.27	2,564	21.8	358.9	3.1	NA	NA	0.42	2.3	.0572	0.9	.377
mVT/Br118.1	0.000153	0.057	0.41	791	77.2	366.7	3.7	NA	NA	0.44	3.2	.0586	1.0	.322
mVT/Br119.1	0.000107	0.056	0.28	1,326	49.9	359.0	3.3	NA	NA	0.43	2.5	.0573	0.9	.377
mVT/Br119.2	0.000063	0.056	0.27	1,811	21.9	363.9	3.2	NA	NA	0.44	1.9	.0582	0.9	.452
mVT/Br120.1	0.000364	0.060	0.75	1,039	62.6	357.5	3.4	NA	NA	0.43	4.2	.0571	1.0	.234
mVT/Br121.1	0.000227	0.057	0.35	668	38.7	365.5	3.8	NA	NA	0.43	3.9	.0583	1.1	.268
mVT/Br122.1	0.000135	0.054	0.08	1,750	29.5	363.3	3.2	NA	NA	0.42	3.0	.0579	0.9	.302
mVT/Br11.1	0.000045	0.054	0.08	3,079	10.3	364.2	3.0	NA	NA	0.43	1.6	.0581	0.8	.535
mVT/Br123.1	0.000454	0.057	0.37	1,528	49.8	361.0	3.3	NA	NA	0.40	4.5	.0573	1.0	.212
mVT/Br123.2	0.000752	0.068	1.81	568	62.7	355.5	4.0	NA	NA	0.45	7.0	.0570	1.2	.172
mVT/Br110.1	0.000134	0.054	-0.02	987	45.8	372.7	3.6	NA	NA	0.42	2.9	.0594	1.0	.341
mVT/Br124.1	0.000355	0.058	0.50	811	125.8	355.1	3.8	NA	NA	0.41	5.4	.0565	1.1	.204
mVT/Br124.2	0.000093	0.056	0.24	1,573	28.8	363.9	3.3	NA	NA	0.44	2.5	.0581	0.9	.369
mVT/Br16.1	0.000091	0.054	0.04	893	44.9	364.9	3.7	NA	NA	0.42	2.9	.0582	1.0	.355
mVT/Br17.1	0.000393	0.058	0.53	666	73.1	364.4	3.7	NA	NA	0.42	4.7	.0580	1.1	.225
mVT/Br18.1	0.000045	0.055	0.22	2,963	15.5	355.8	2.9	NA	NA	0.43	1.5	.0568	0.8	.557
mVT/Br125.1	0.000273	0.055	0.13	1,310	47.8	364.9	3.3	NA	NA	0.41	3.4	.0580	0.9	.271
mVT/Br125.2	0.001054	0.070	1.95	716	49.3	367.2	3.7	NA	NA	0.44	7.9	.0586	1.1	.140
mVT/Br19.1	0.000921	0.061	0.85	302	117.8	377.6	4.7	NA	NA	0.39	11.1	.0598	1.4	.124
						VT/Pl 2–91 (Granite dike south of Plymouth)								
VT/Pl1–1.1	0.000033	.0790	-0.11	315	0.38	1,195.4	24.8	NA	NA	2.20	2.7	.2034	2.1	.782
VT/Pl1–2.1	—	.0847	0.15	225	0.35	1,279.5	26.9	NA	NA	2.57	2.5	.2199	2.2	.879
VT/Pl1–3.1	0.000096	.0860	0.26	155	0.39	1,288.5	27.8	NA	NA	2.59	2.7	.2215	2.2	.823
VT/Pl1–4.1	—	.0543	0.00	47	0.02	383.9	13.5	NA	NA	0.46	6.9	.0614	3.6	.517
VT/Pl1–5.1	—	.0575	0.31	288	0.04	411.0	9.0	NA	NA	0.52	3.3	.0660	2.2	.667
VT/Pl1–5.2	—	.0855	0.48	359	0.31	1,232.2	25.4	NA	NA	2.50	2.3	.2117	2.1	.925
VT/Pl1–6.1	—	.0759	-0.33	267	0.55	1,165.9	26.5	NA	NA	2.07	2.6	.1976	2.4	.901
VT/Pl1–7.1	0.000102	.0549	0.06	527	0.01	387.1	8.2	NA	NA	0.46	3.1	.0618	2.2	.699
VT/Pl1–8.1	—	.0550	0.14	79	0.01	366.3	9.0	NA	NA	0.44	7.1	.0586	2.5	.344
VT/Pl1–9.1	—	.0740	0.13	197	0.03	1,010.6	21.3	NA	NA	1.73	2.6	.1699	2.2	.843
VT/Pl1–10.1	—	.0727	0.18	485	0.06	963.9	19.8	NA	NA	1.62	2.3	.1616	2.1	.915
VT/Pl1–11.1	0.000271	.0594	0.63	3,187	0.23	384.4	7.9	NA	NA	0.47	2.4	.0615	2.1	.858
VT/Pl1–12.1	0.001328	.0726	2.31	556	0.05	368.2	7.8	NA	NA	0.43	6.7	.0587	2.2	.327

Table 3. Sensitive high resolution ion microprobe (SHRIMP) uranium-thorium-lead (U-Th-Pb) data for zircon and monazite from rocks of Vermont.—Continued

[Abbreviations are as follows: Ma, millions of years (mega-annum); NA, not applicable; ppm, parts per million; —, measured ^{204}Pb below detection limit; ρ, error correlation]

Analysis[1]	Measured ^{204}Pb/^{206}Pb	Measured ^{207}Pb/^{206}Pb	Percent common ^{206}Pb	Uranium (ppm)	Th/U	^{206}Pb/^{238}U (Ma)[2]	Error (Ma)[3]	^{207}Pb/^{206}Pb (Ma)[2]	Error (Ma)[3]	^{207}Pb/^{235}U[4]	Error (percent)[3]	^{206}Pb/^{238}U[4]	Error (percent)[3]	ρ
						VT/Pl 2–91 (Granite dike south of Plymouth)—Continued								
VT/Pl1–13.1	0.007440	.1525	12.18	3,609	0.25	379.0	12.5	NA	NA	0.35	80.0	.0597	3.9	.048
VT/Pl1–14.1	0.001482	.0727	2.35	645	0.21	363.3	7.9	NA	NA	0.41	13.7	.0578	2.3	.171
VT/Pl1–16.1	0.004493	.1171	7.82	214	0.02	371.7	9.8	NA	NA	0.42	42.2	.0592	3.2	.076
VT/Pl1–17.1	—	.0666	0.81	253	0.19	603.1	13.1	NA	NA	0.91	3.0	.0989	2.2	.755

[1]The prefix "m" for analyses of sample VT/Br 1–89 means monazite; all other samples are zircon; labels for individual analyses may be abbreviated.

[2] ^{206}Pb/^{238}U and ^{207}Pb/^{206}Pb ages are corrected for common lead using the ^{204}Pb-correction method, which is based on a model by Stacey and Kramers (1975). Decay constants from Steiger and Jäger (1977).

[3]1σ errors.

[4]Radiogenic ratios, corrected for common lead using the ^{204}Pb-correction method, which is based on the model by Stacey and Kramers (1975).

20

Table 4. Thermal ionization mass spectrometry (TIMS) uranium-lead (U-Pb) data for zircon from rocks of Vermont.

[Abbreviations: A, abraded; C, colorless; E, elongate; Ma, millions of years (mega-annum); mg, milligrams; Mg, magnetic; NMD, nonmagnetic, diamagnetic; Pb, lead; ppm, parts per million; U, uranium. The term "dust" refers to rim material removed by abrasion]

Fraction	Weight (mg)	Concentrations (ppm)		206Pb/204Pb[1]	Ratios (percent error)[2]			Ages (Ma)[3,4]		
		U	Pb		206Pb/238U	207Pb/235U	207Pb/206Pb	206Pb/238U	207Pb/235U	207Pb/206Pb
VT/Pe 2-88 (Bondville metadacite at Winhall River bridge)										
(-100+150) NMDA	0.42	148.6	33.07	1648.5	0.2197 (0.20)	2.573 (0.22)	0.0849 (0.10)	1280	1293	1314
(+100)NMDEA	0.21	221.3	49.81	1115.8	0.2295 (0.15)	2.738 (0.22)	0.0865 (0.14)	1332	1339	1350
(-100+150) NMDEA	0.69	286.9	54.63	3865.0	0.1902 (0.15)	2.171 (0.17)	0.0828 (0.07)	1122	1172	1264
(-100+150) NMDEA	0.51	179.9	40.08	1344.5	0.2176 (0.42)	2.576 (0.44)	0.0858 (0.12)	1269	1294	1335
(-100+150) NMDEA	0.41	219.3	49.17	1367.9	0.2207 (0.15)	2.593 (0.20)	0.0852 (0.12)	1285	1299	1320
(+100) Dust	0.61	170.0	30.73	438.3	0.1709 (0.15)	1.893 (0.25)	0.0803 (0.17)	1017	1079	1205
(-100+150) Dust	0.44	214.0	40.48	1055.3	0.1912 (0.15)	2.150 (0.23)	0.0815 (0.17)	1128	1165	1235
(-100+150) Dust	0.06	1990	80.44	185.24	0.1557 (0.36)	1.665 (0.81)	0.0776 (0.64)	933	995	1136
(-100+150) Dust	0.10	167.9	32.72	192.91	0.1787 (0.42)	1.928 (0.94)	0.0783 (0.75)	1060	1091	1153
(-100+150) Dust	0.10	124.8	20.05	106.98	0.1278 (0.77)	1.356 (01.8)	0.0770 (01.4)	775	870	1120
(-100+150) Dust	0.28	179.4	31.1	411.78	0.1696 (0.83)	1.831 (0.90)	0.0783 (0.31)	1010	1057	1155
87Rat-2 (College Hill Granite Gneiss at Stratton Mountain)										
(-50+100) NMDA	1.15	221.1	49.43	433.76	0.2014 (0.48)	2.271 (0.49)	0.0818 (0.11)	1183	1203	1240
(-50+100) NMDAMg	0.87	217.6	39.25	626.87	0.1712 (0.54)	1.941 (0.54)	0.0823 (0.08)	1019	1095	1252
(-100+150) NMDA	0.92	205.0	43.48	226.99	0.2017 (0.66)	2.280 (0.65)	0.0820 (0.23)	1184	1206	1245
(-100+150) NMDAMg	0.90	220.2	46.85	214.97	0.2051 (0.70)	2.313 (0.69)	0.0818 (0.27)	1203	1216	1241
(-150+200) NMDA	1.93	303.8	61.55	1467.2	0.2001 (0.47)	2.215 (0.47)	0.0803 (0.06)	1176	1186	1205
(-150+200) NMDAMg	1.84	320.5	69.59	530.86	0.1988 (0.47)	2.201 (0.48)	0.0803 (0.10)	1169	1181	1204
(-200+250) NMD	4.10	329.5	65.14	1050.8	0.1924 (0.47)	2.098 (0.47)	0.0791 (0.06)	1135	1148	1174
(-400)	0.87	329.1	64.38	651.17	0.1869 (0.47)	2.022 (0.49)	0.0785 (0.13)	1105	1123	1159
(-50+100) Dust	0.24	183.9	30.40	339.2	0.1719 (0.58)	1.805 (0.61)	0.0761 (0.26)	1023	1047	1099
VT/Lo 1-89 (granitic gneiss)										
(-100+150) NMDEA	0.65	156.7	31.97	3284.5	0.2038 (0.24)	2.271 (0.25)	0.0808 (0.08)	1196	1203	1217
(-100+150) NMDEA	0.72	174.9	35.38	4199.5	0.2025 (0.15)	2.249 (0.17)	0.0806 (0.07)	1187	1196	1211
(-150+200) NMDEA	0.37	201.8	42.60	3168.1	0.2132 (0.18)	2.377 (0.21)	0.0808 (0.09)	1246	1236	1218
(-150+200) NMDEA	0.47	197.3	40.18	2289.8	0.2055 (0.13)	2.278 (0.15)	0.0805 (0.08)	1205	1206	1208
(-150+200) NMDEA	0.34	187.2	37.91	3187.0	0.2045 (0.12)	2.277 (0.14)	0.0808 (0.07)	1200	1205	1216
(-100+150) Dust	0.17	137.8	31.19	176.92	0.1856 (0.31)	1.978 (0.68)	0.0773 (0.54)	1097	1108	1128

21

Table 4. Thermal ionization mass spectrometry (TIMS) uranium-lead (U-Pb) data for zircon from rocks of Vermont.—Continued

[Abbreviations: A, abraded; C, colorless; E, elongate; Ma, millions of years (mega-annum); mg, milligrams; Mg, magnetic; NMD, nonmagnetic, diamagnetic; Pb, lead; ppm, parts per million; U, uranium. The term "dust" refers to rim material removed by abrasion]

Fraction	Weight (mg)	Concentrations (ppm)		206Pb/204Pb[1]	Ratios (percent error)[2]			Ages (Ma)[3,4]		
		U	Pb		206Pb/238U	207Pb/235U	207Pb/206Pb	206Pb/238U	207Pb/235U	207Pb/206Pb
SR3053 (Tonalite gneiss in the North River Igneous Suite)										
(-100+150) ECA	0.011	294.8	31.00	237.79	0.0763 (0.55)	0.5975 (0.70)	0.0568 (0.42)	473.8	475.6	484.5
(-100+150) ECA	0.014	372.5	33.39	1020.5	0.0770 (0.26)	0.6034 (0.31)	0.0569 (0.16)	477.9	479.4	486.3
(-100+150) ECA	0.016	302.8	29.95	256.66	0.0792 (0.93)	0.6260 (1.1)	0.0573 (0.55)	491.3	493.6	504.2
(-100+150) ECA	0.026	278.1	25.17	514.9	0.0770 (0.68)	0.6033 (0.81)	0.0568 (0.42)	478.4	479.3	483.8
(-100+150) ECA	0.017	298.7	35.41	139.80	0.0772 (0.87)	0.6100 (1.15)	0.0573 (0.71)	479.4	483.5	503.4
(-100+150) ECA	0.011	381.8	34.99	472.60	0.0771 (0.58)	0.6041 (0.70)	0.0569 (0.38)	478.5	479.8	486.1
(-100+150) ECA	0.024	347.3	30.49	831.88	0.7677 (0.62)	0.6025 (0.73)	0.0569 (0.35)	476.8	478.9	488.7
(-100+150) ECA	0.010	433.1	47.48	164.51	0.7655 (1.05)	0.5995 (1.28)	0.0568 (0.71)	475.5	476.9	483.8

[1]Measured ratio.

[2]2σ errors.

[3]Corrected for common lead using appropriate values from Stacey and Kramers (1975).

[4]Decay constants used for age calculation from Steiger and Jäger (1977).

Sample number: 1
Description: Hornblende diorite gneiss at South Londonderry
Field number: Lon–1–A
Method: SHRIMP
Age: 1,393±9 Ma
Sample location coordinates (WGS 84 datum): 43°11′06″N., 72°48′09″W.
Sample location description: In bed of the West River, 0.7 km southeast of South Londonderry in the Londonderry quadrangle.

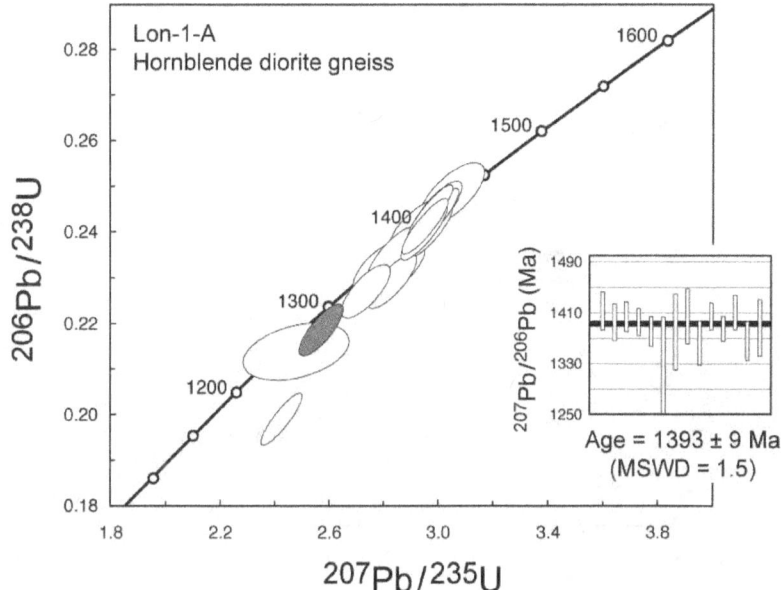

Figure 1. Conventional concordia plot of SHRIMP U-Pb data for zircon from hornblende diorite gneiss at South Londonderry, Vermont. White-filled error ellipses represent data from oscillatory-zoned cores used in the weighted average calculation of $^{207}Pb/^{206}Pb$ ages (see inset) for determining the time of emplacement of the igneous protolith. Gray error ellipse represents an analysis that overlapped an igneous core and metamorphic rim, yielding a geologically meaningless mixed age. Abbreviations are as follows: km, kilometers; Ma, millions of years (mega-annum); MSWD, mean square of the weighted deviates; SHRIMP, sensitive high resolution ion microprobe; WGS 84, World Geodetic System datum of 1984.

Sample number: 2
Description: Baileys Mills tonalitic gneiss in the Chester dome
Field number: VT–CSTR–1
Method: SHRIMP
Age: 1,383±13 Ma
Sample location coordinates (WGS 84 datum): 43°19'10"N., 72°36'29"W.
Sample location description: Roadcut on the eastern side of Vermont Route 103, about 600 m south of the intersection with Vermont Route 10 in the Chester quadrangle.

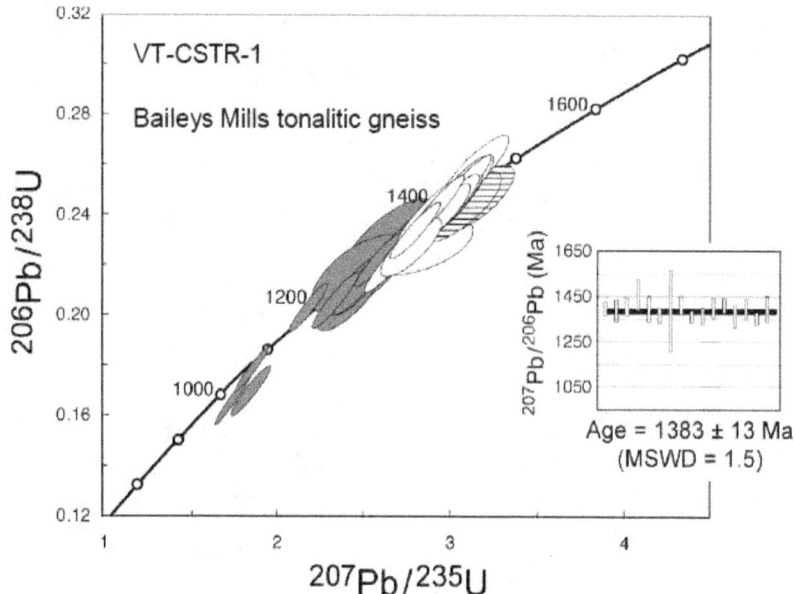

Figure 2. Conventional concordia plot of SHRIMP U-Pb data for zircon from tonalitic gneiss at Baileys Mills, Vermont. White-filled error ellipses represent data from oscillatory-zoned cores used in the weighted average calculation of $^{207}Pb/^{206}Pb$ ages (see inset) for determining the time of emplacement of the igneous protolith. Gray error ellipses represent data from metamorphic rims (dark, unzoned in CL; approx. 1.05, 1.17–1.31 Ga). Horizontally ruled ellipses represent older ages (approx. 1.5 Ga) in cores from inherited zircon. Abbreviations are as follows: approx., approximately; CL, cathodoluminescence; Ga, billions of years (giga-annum); m, meters; Ma, millions of years (mega-annum); MSWD, mean square of the weighted deviates; SHRIMP, sensitive high resolution ion microprobe; WGS 84, World Geodetic System datum of 1984.

Sample number: 3
Description: Rawsonville trondhjemite gneiss at Bromley Mountain
Field number: VT/Pe 1–88 (6327)
Method: SHRIMP
Age: 1,367±16 Ma
Sample location coordinates (WGS 84 datum): 43°13′40″N., 72°56′26″W.
Sample location description: Sample collected near the top of Bromley Mountain in the Peru quadrangle, approximately 7 m south of the top of the ski lift.

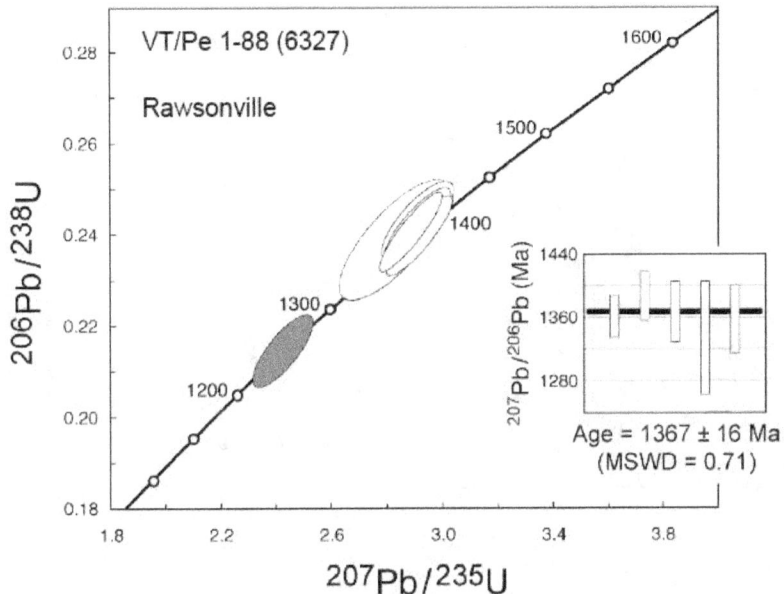

Figure 3. Conventional concordia plot of SHRIMP U-Pb data for zircon from Rawsonville trondhjemite gneiss at Bromley Mountain, Vermont. White-filled error ellipses represent data from oscillatory-zoned cores used in the weighted average calculation of $^{207}Pb/^{206}Pb$ ages (see inset) for determining the time of emplacement of the igneous protolith. Gray error ellipse represents an analysis of a damaged area (crack) within a core, resulting in lead loss; age probably is geologically meaningless. Previous discordant TIMS data (Ratcliffe and others, 1991) suggested an age of 1,356.5±2.7 Ma for this sample. Abbreviations are as follows: m, meters; Ma, millions of years (mega-annum); MSWD, mean square of the weighted deviates; SHRIMP, sensitive high resolution ion microprobe; TIMS, thermal ionization mass spectrometry; WGS 84, World Geodetic System datum of 1984.

Sample number: 4
Description: Felchville Gneiss (aplite facies) at Cavendish Gorge
Field number: C718
Method: SHRIMP
Age: 1,372±11 Ma
Sample location coordinates (WGS 84 datum): 43°23′04″N., 72°35′54″W.
Sample location description: Southern side of the power station at Cavendish Gorge in sharp contact with underlying dolomite marble of the Cavendish Formation in the Cavendish quadrangle.

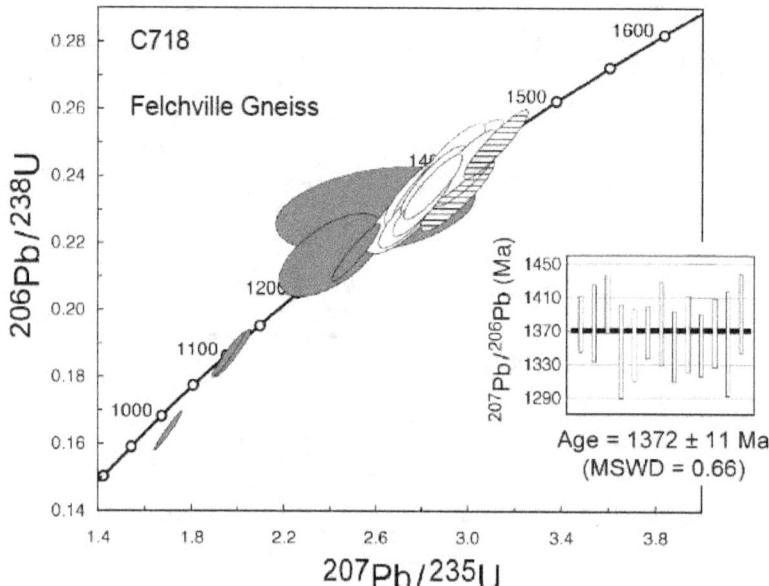

Figure 4. Conventional concordia plot of SHRIMP U-Pb data for zircon from Felchville Gneiss (aplite facies) from Cavendish Gorge, Vermont. White-filled error ellipses represent data from oscillatory-zoned cores used in the weighted average calculation of ^{207}Pb/^{206}Pb ages (see inset) for determining the time of emplacement of the igneous protolith. Gray error ellipses represent data from metamorphic rims (dark, unzoned in CL; approx. 1.06–1.09, 1.21–1.29 Ga). Horizontally ruled ellipses represent older ages (approx. 1.45 Ga) in cores from inherited zircon. Abbreviations are as follows: approx., approximately; Ga, billions of years (giga-annum); Ma, millions of years (mega-annum); MSWD, mean square of the weighted deviates; SHRIMP, sensitive high resolution ion microprobe; WGS 84, World Geodetic System datum of 1984.

Sample number: 5
Description: Felchville Gneiss (trondhjemite facies) at Felchville
Field number: C609
Method: SHRIMP
Age: 1,370±11 Ma
Sample location coordinates (WGS 84 datum): 43°28'10"N., 72°32'00"W.
Sample location description: Roadcut on the western side of Vermont Route 106, opposite its intersection with Vermont Route 44 in the Cavendish quadrangle.

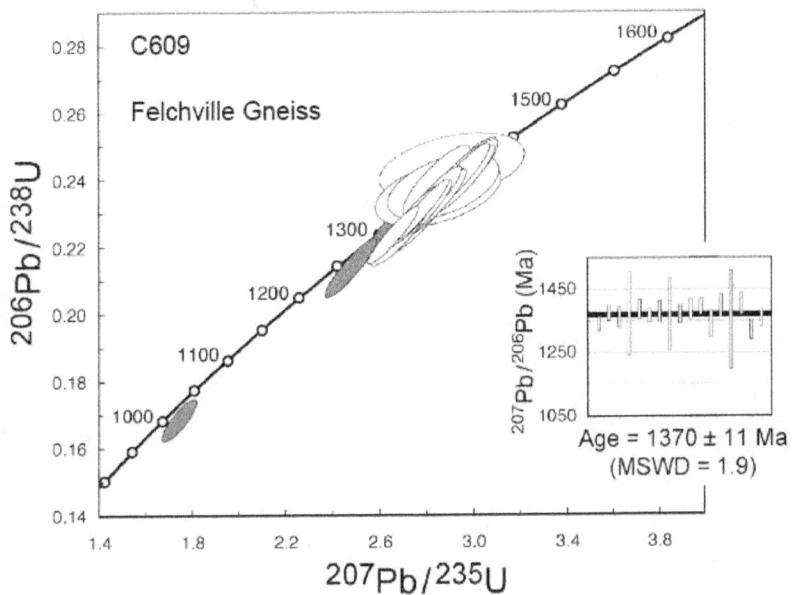

Figure 5. Conventional concordia plot of SHRIMP U-Pb data for zircon from Felchville Gneiss (trondhjemite facies) from Felchville, Vermont. White-filled error ellipses represent data from oscillatory-zoned cores used in the weighted average calculation of $^{207}Pb/^{206}Pb$ ages (see inset) for determining the time of emplacement of the igneous protolith. Gray error ellipses represent data from metamorphic rims (dark, unzoned in CL; approx. 1.06, 1.29–1.31 Ga). One rim (not shown) has an age of about 500 Ma. Abbreviations are as follows: approx., approximately; CL, cathodoluminescence; Ga, billions of years (giga-annum); Ma, millions of years (mega-annum); MSWD, mean square of the weighted deviates; SHRIMP, sensitive high resolution ion microprobe; WGS 84, World Geodetic System datum of 1984.

Sample number: 6B

Description: Bondville metadacite at Winhall River bridge

Field number: VT/Pe 2–88 (6329)

Method: TIMS

Age: approx. 1,342 Ma

Sample location coordinates (WGS 84 datum): 43°08′40″N., 72°52′34″W.

Sample location description: Winhall River bridge on Vermont Route 30, Bondville, Vt. Sample collected from a pavement outcrop exposed at the base of the eastern bridge abutment during construction.

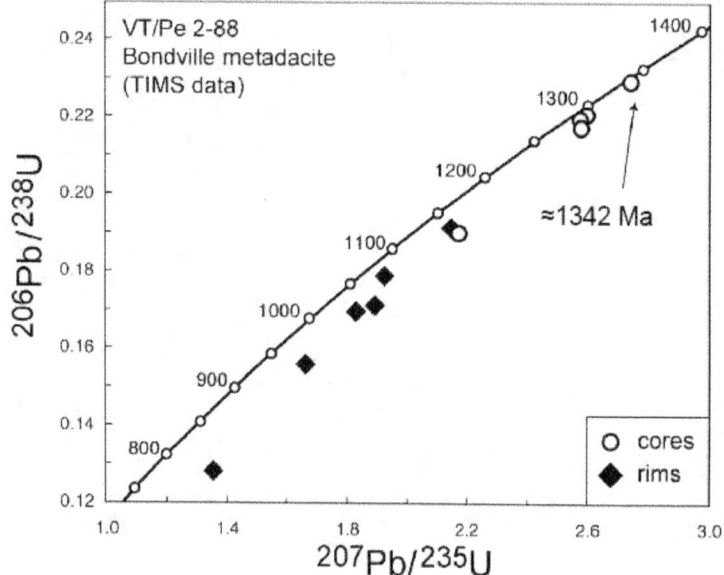

Figure 6.   Conventional concordia plot of TIMS U-Pb data for zircon from Bondville metadacite at Winhall River bridge in Bondville, Vermont. White-filled circles represent data from cores (some of which were in Ratcliffe and others, 1991); black-filled diamonds represent material removed by abrasion. Because most of the data are discordant, the best estimate of the age of this rock is the $^{207}Pb/^{206}Pb$ age of the least discordant fraction (approx. 1,342 Ma). Abbreviations are as follows: ≈, approximately; Ma, millions of years (mega-annum); TIMS, thermal ionization mass spectrometry; WGS 84, World Geodetic System datum of 1984.

Sample number: 7
Description: Cole Pond tonalite gneiss
Field number: 87Rat–1 (3016A)
Method: SHRIMP
Age: 1,321±9 Ma
Sample location coordinates (WGS 84 datum): 43°08′37″N., 72°48′38″W.
Sample location description: Roadcuts on the western side of Cole Pond Road, a dirt road leading to Cole Pond from Vermont Route 100, approximately 160 m southwest of Cole Pond in the Londonderry quadrangle.

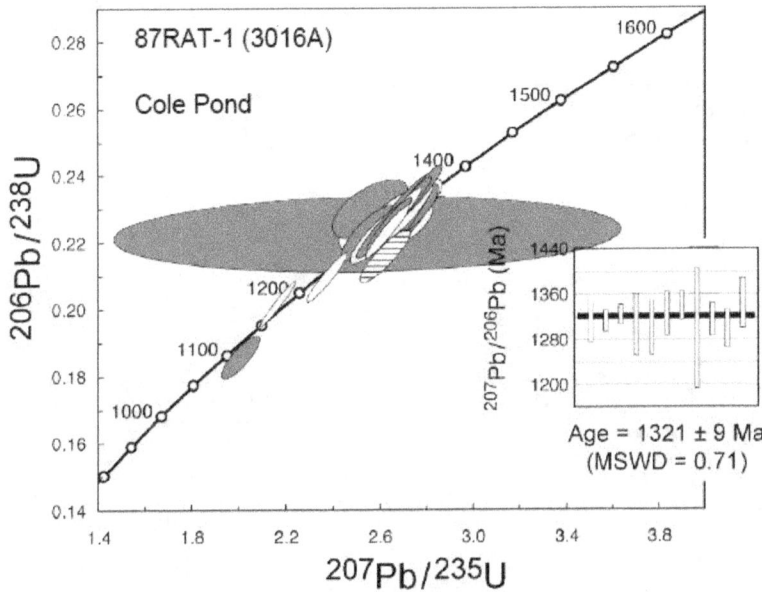

Figure 7. Conventional concordia plot of SHRIMP U-Pb data for zircon from Cole Pond tonalite gneiss near Cole Pond, Vermont. White-filled error ellipses represent data from oscillatory-zoned cores; gray error ellipses represent data from metamorphic rims (dark, unzoned in CL). $^{207}Pb/^{206}Pb$ weighted average age is calculated from cores only. Close agreement of ages of cores and rims at about 1.31 Ga suggests synmetamorphic emplacement of the trondhjemite. Horizontally ruled ellipse represents an older age (approx. 1.38 Ga) from inherited zircon. Previous discordant TIMS data (Ratcliffe and others, 1991) suggested an age of 1,308±10 Ma for this sample. Abbreviations are as follows: approx., approximately; CL, cathodoluminescence; Ga, billions of years (giga-annum); m, meters; Ma, millions of years (mega-annum); MSWD, mean square of the weighted deviates; SHRIMP, sensitive high resolution ion microprobe; TIMS, thermal ionization mass spectrometry; WGS 84, World Geodetic System datum of 1984.

Sample number: 8

Description: Migmatite gneiss at Stratton Mountain

Field number: VT/Ja 1–88

Method: SHRIMP

Age: 1,326±4 Ma

Sample location coordinates (WGS 84 datum): 43°05′14″N., 72°53′14″W.

Sample location description: Roadcut on Mountain Road about 0.5 km northwest of Forester Pond near the western border of the Jamaica quadrangle and south of 597.2-m benchmark.

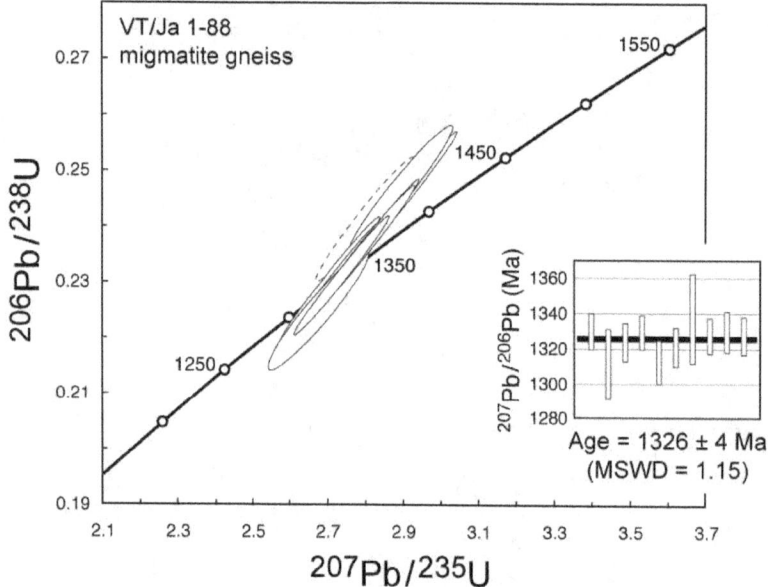

Figure 8. Conventional concordia plot of SHRIMP U-Pb data for zircon from migmatite gneiss at Stratton Mountain, Vermont. White-filled error ellipses represent data from oscillatory-zoned cores used in the weighted average calculation of ^{207}Pb/^{206}Pb ages (see inset) for determining the time of emplacement of the igneous protolith. Dashed outline of error ellipse represents reversely discordant data, possibly from damaged area of grain. Abbreviations are as follows: m, meters; Ma, millions of years (mega-annum); MSWD, mean square of the weighted deviates; SHRIMP, sensitive high resolution ion microprobe; WGS 84, World Geodetic System datum of 1984.

Sample number: 9
Description: Fine-grained granodiorite of the Ludlow Mountain granodiorite gneiss at Okemo Mountain
Field number: VT/Lu 1–91
Method: SHRIMP
Age: 1,309±6 Ma
Sample location coordinates (WGS 84 datum): 43°24'37"N., 72°44'36"W.
Sample location description: Sample collected from blasted outcrop at the summit of Ludlow Mountain at the top of Okemo ski area, on a dirt road from the top descending to a ski lift, in the Ludlow quadrangle.

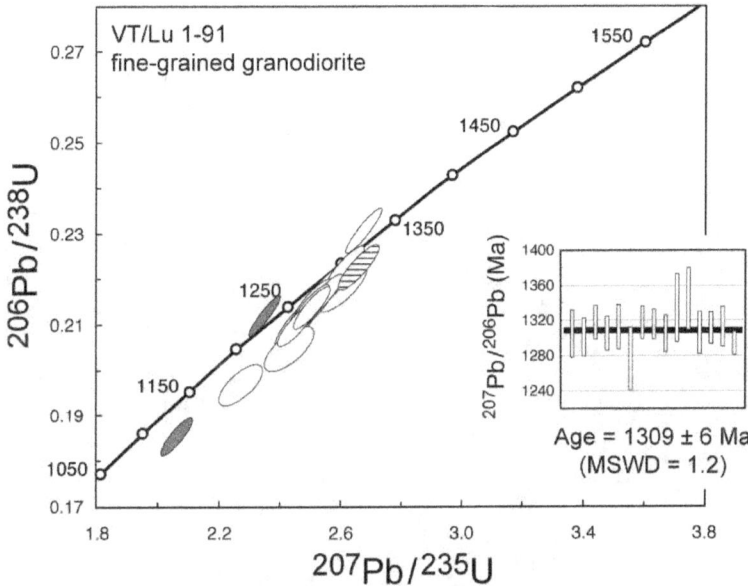

Figure 9. Conventional concordia plot of SHRIMP U-Pb data for zircon from fine-grained granodiorite of the Ludlow Mountain granodiorite gneiss at Ludlow Mountain, Vermont. No CL available at time of analyses (1996). White-filled error ellipses represent data from interiors of grains used in the weighted average calculation of $^{207}Pb/^{206}Pb$ ages (see inset) for determining the time of emplacement of the igneous protolith. Gray error ellipses represent data from edges (metamorphic rims?) of grains (approx. 1.20 Ga). Horizontally ruled ellipse represents older age (approx. 1.34 Ga) in interior of grain, probably from inherited zircon. One older grain (approx. 1.64 Ga) not shown. Abbreviations are as follows: approx., approximately; CL, cathodoluminescence; Ma, millions of years (mega-annum); MSWD, mean square of the weighted deviates; SHRIMP, sensitive high resolution ion microprobe; WGS 84, World Geodetic System datum of 1984.

Sample number: 10
Description: Okemo Quartzite—Detrital zircon
Field number: Vt/Lu 2–91
Method: SHRIMP
Age: about 1,261 to 1,359 Ma
Sample location coordinates (WGS 84 datum): 43°24′55″N., 72°44′29″W.
Sample location description: Sample collected at a small roadcut about 1.6 km north of the Ludlow Mountain summit at Okemo ski area, on the paved summit road, in the Ludlow quadrangle.

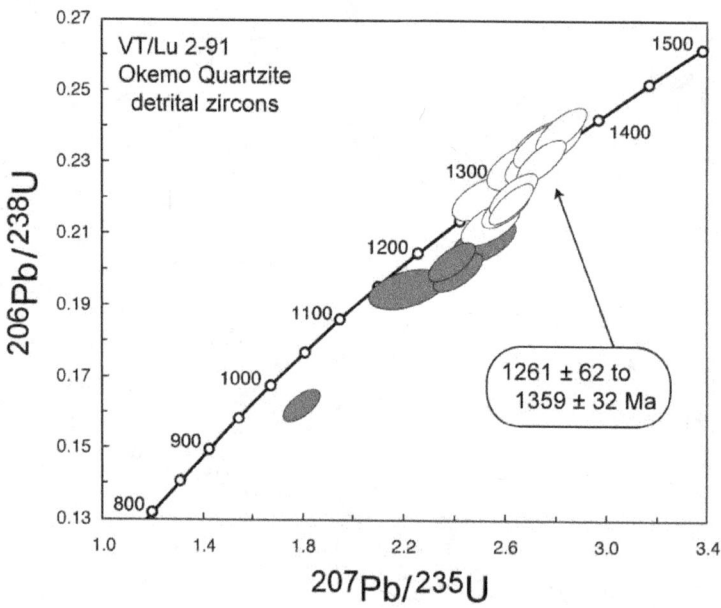

Figure 10. Conventional concordia plot of SHRIMP U-Pb data for detrital zircon from Okemo Quartzite at Ludlow Mountain, Vermont. All analyses from oscillatory-zoned cores. White-filled error ellipses represent concordant or less than 10 percent discordant analyses. Gray error ellipses represent discordant data. Abbreviations are as follows: km, kilometers; Ma, millions of years (mega-annum); SHRIMP, sensitive high resolution ion microprobe; WGS 84, World Geodetic System datum of 1984.

Sample number: 11
Description: College Hill Granite Gneiss at Stratton Mountain
Field number: 87Rat–2
Method: TIMS
Age: 1,244±8 Ma
Sample location coordinates (WGS 84 datum): 43°07'37"N., 72°52'15"W.
Sample location description: Exposure in woods near Pearl Buck Drive, 400 m west of the boundary between Bennington and Windsor Counties in the southwestern corner of the Jamaica quadrangle.

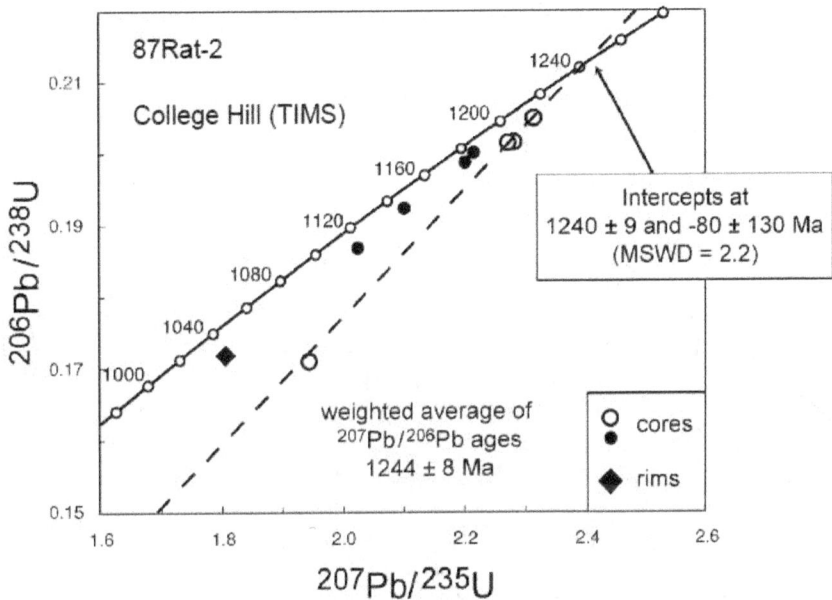

Figure 11. Conventional concordia plot of TIMS U-Pb data for zircon from College Hill Granite Gneiss at Stratton Mountain, Vermont. Circles represent data from cores; black-filled diamond represents material removed by abrasion. Best-fit regression (dashed line) is calculated through four analyses of cores (white-filled circles), yielding an upper intercept age of 1,240±9 Ma. The weighted average of [207]Pb/[206]Pb ages from these four fractions is 1,244±8 Ma (preferred age). Black dots probably represent mixtures of cores and rims. Black diamond suggests presence of metamorphic overgrowths. Abbreviations are as follows: m, meters; Ma, millions of years (mega-annum); MSWD, mean square of the weighted deviates; TIMS, thermal ionization mass spectrometry; WGS 84, World Geodetic System datum of 1984.

Sample number: 12
Description: Granitic gneiss, which crosscuts older and deformed intrusive rocks (suite ranging in age from 1.3 to 1.4 Ga) and paragneiss
Field number: VT/Lo 1–89
Method: TIMS
Age: 1,221±4 Ma
Sample location coordinates (WGS 84 datum): 43°11′19″N., 72°52′15″W.
Sample location description: Western side of Winhall Hollow Road between Peru and Landgrove, north of French Hollow Road.

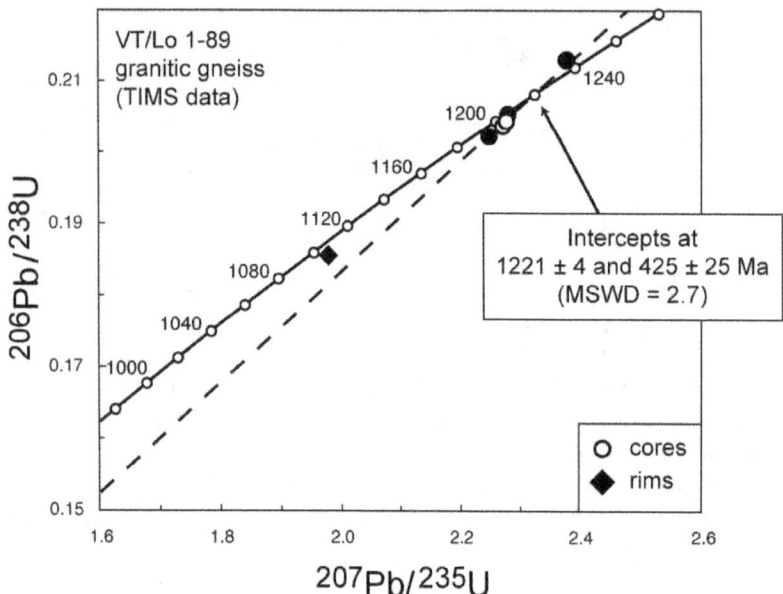

Figure 12. Conventional concordia plot of TIMS U-Pb data for zircon from granitic gneiss. Circles represent data from cores; black-filled diamond represents material removed by abrasion. Best-fit regression (dashed line), forced through a regionally reasonable lower intercept age of 425±25 Ma, is calculated through two analyses of cores (white-filled circles), yielding an upper intercept age of 1,221±4 Ma. Black dots represent slightly younger ages, probably the result of mixtures of cores and rims. Black diamond suggests presence of metamorphic overgrowths. Abbreviations are as follows: m, meters; Ma, millions of years (mega-annum); MSWD, mean square of the weighted deviates; TIMS, thermal ionization mass spectrometry; WGS 84, World Geodetic System datum of 1984.

Sample number: 13

Description: Megacrystic augen gneiss at Brandon Gap

Field number: MC6000

Method: SHRIMP

Age: 1,149±8 Ma

Sample location coordinates (WGS 84 datum): 43°50′24″N., 72°58′03″W.

Sample location description: Roadcut located on the northern side of Vermont Route 73, about 15 m west of the Long Trail, at the summit of Brandon Gap.

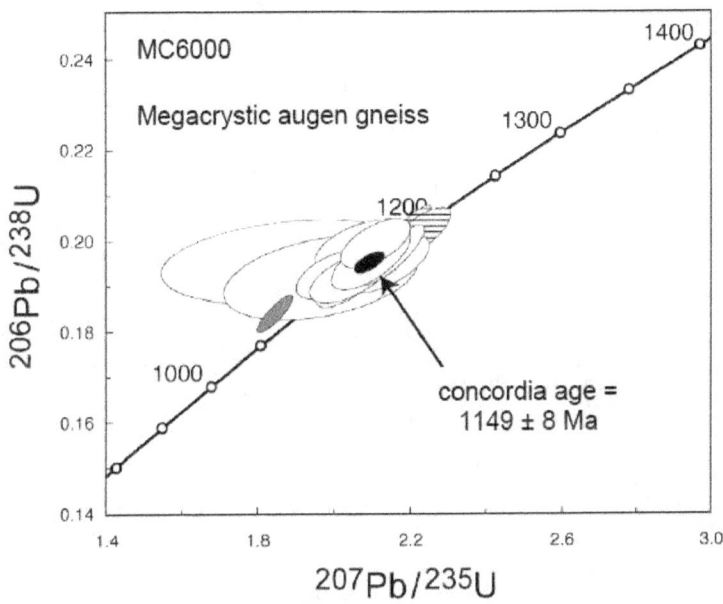

Figure 13. Conventional concordia plot of SHRIMP U-Pb data for zircon from megacrystic augen gneiss at Brandon Gap, Vermont. Concordia age is calculated for data from oscillatory-zoned cores, represented by white-filled error ellipses (*n*=15). Two slightly older analyses (horizontally ruled ellipses; approx. 1.16, 1.19 Ga) excluded from age calculation suggest minor inheritance. Gray error ellipse represents reversely discordant data from metamorphic rim (dark, unzoned in CL; approx. 1.00 Ga). Abbreviations are as follows: approx., approximately; CL, cathodoluminescence; Ga, billions of years (giga-annum); m, meters; Ma, millions of years (mega-annum); SHRIMP, sensitive high resolution ion microprobe; WGS 84, World Geodetic System datum of 1984.

Sample number: 16
Description: Migmatite gneiss in Pine Hill slice
Field number: R2008
Method: SHRIMP
Age: 1,037±6 Ma
Sample location coordinates (WGS 84 datum): 43°23′40″N., 73°05′00″W.
Sample location description: At the Pike Industries quarry property. The outcrop is located on a forested east-facing slope, just west of the runaway truck ramp, about 200 m west of U.S. Route 7.

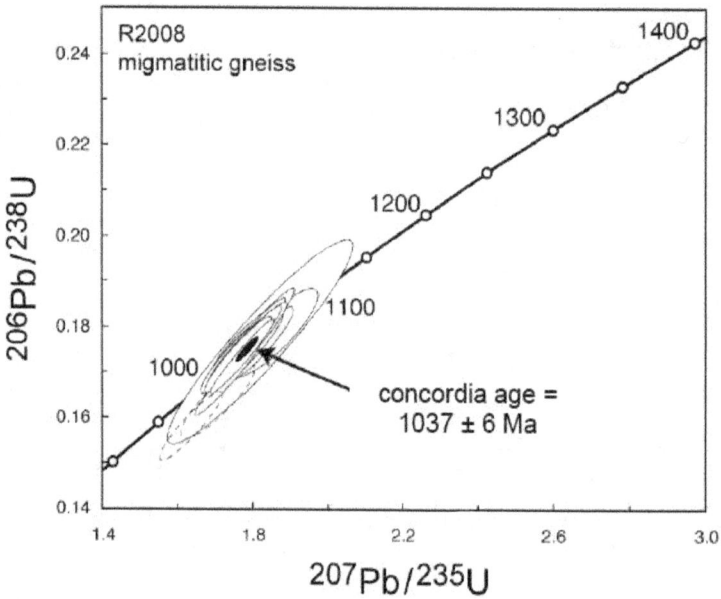

Figure 14. Conventional concordia plot of SHRIMP U-Pb data for zircon from migmatite gneiss in the Pine Hill slice, Vermont. Concordia age is calculated for data from oscillatory-zoned cores, represented by white-filled error ellipses (*n*=17). Two slightly discordant analyses (dashed outlines of error ellipses) excluded from age calculation, suggest minor lead loss. Abbreviations are as follows: m, meters; Ma, millions of years (mega-annum); SHRIMP, sensitive high resolution ion microprobe; WGS 84, World Geodetic System datum of 1984.

Sample number: 22
Description: Newfane tonalite, which intrudes the Cram Hill Formation near South Newfane
Field number: VT/Br 2–89
Method: SHRIMP
Age: 502±4 Ma
Sample location coordinates (WGS 84 datum): 42°56'00"N., 72°42'24"W.
Sample location description: Roadcut on Auger Hole Road about 350 m south of road junction in South Newfane, Newfane quadrangle.

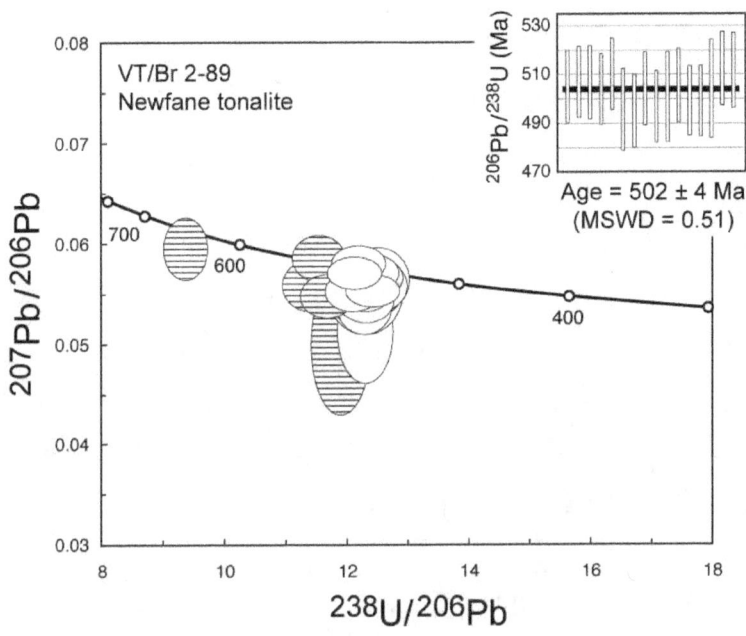

Figure 15. Tera-Wasserburg concordia plot of SHRIMP U-Pb data for zircon from Newfane tonalite near South Newfane, Vermont. White-filled error ellipses represent data from oscillatory-zoned cores used in the weighted average calculation of $^{206}Pb/^{238}U$ ages (see inset) for determining the time of emplacement of the igneous protolith. Horizontally ruled ellipses represent older ages (approx. 520–550, 650 Ma; 1,520-Ma analysis not shown) in cores from inherited zircon. Abbreviations are as follows: approx., approximately; m, meters; Ma, millions of years (mega-annum); MSWD, mean square of the weighted deviates; SHRIMP, sensitive high resolution ion microprobe; WGS 84, World Geodetic System datum of 1984.

Sample number: 23
Description: Trondhjemite in the Barnard Gneiss proper (of Richardson, 1924) north of Proctorsville
Field number: L–18
Method: SHRIMP
Age: 496±8 Ma
Sample location coordinates (WGS 84 datum): 43°25′24″N., 72°38′12″W.
Sample location description: Outcrop in the woods about 200 m south of a powerline cut, about 5 km north of Proctorsville, in the Ludlow quadrangle.

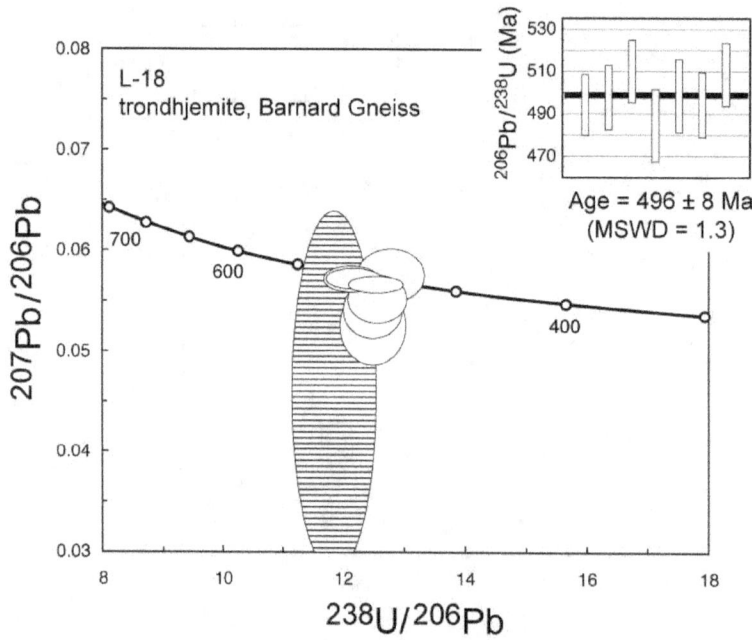

Figure 16. Tera-Wasserburg concordia plot of SHRIMP U-Pb data for zircon from trondhjemite in the Barnard Gneiss proper (of Richardson, 1924) north of Proctorsville, Vermont. White-filled error ellipses represent data from oscillatory-zoned cores used in the weighted average calculation of $^{206}Pb/^{238}U$ ages (see inset) for determining the time of emplacement of the igneous protolith. Horizontally ruled ellipse represents older age (approx. 530 Ma; 1,260-Ma analysis not shown) in core from inherited zircon. Abbreviations are as follows: approx., approximately; km, kilometers; m, meters; Ma, millions of years (mega-annum); MSWD, mean square of the weighted deviates; SHRIMP, sensitive high resolution ion microprobe; WGS 84, World Geodetic System datum of 1984.

Sample number: 24
Description: Tonalite gneiss in the North River Igneous Suite near Bartonsville
Field number: SR3053
Method: TIMS
Age: 486±3 Ma
Sample location coordinates (WGS 84 datum): 43°14'17"N., 72°32'34"W.
Sample location description: Outcrop in the woods near the top of a hill, about 1.5 km north-northwest of Bartonsville and about 100 m west of Whitney Road, in the Saxtons River quadrangle.

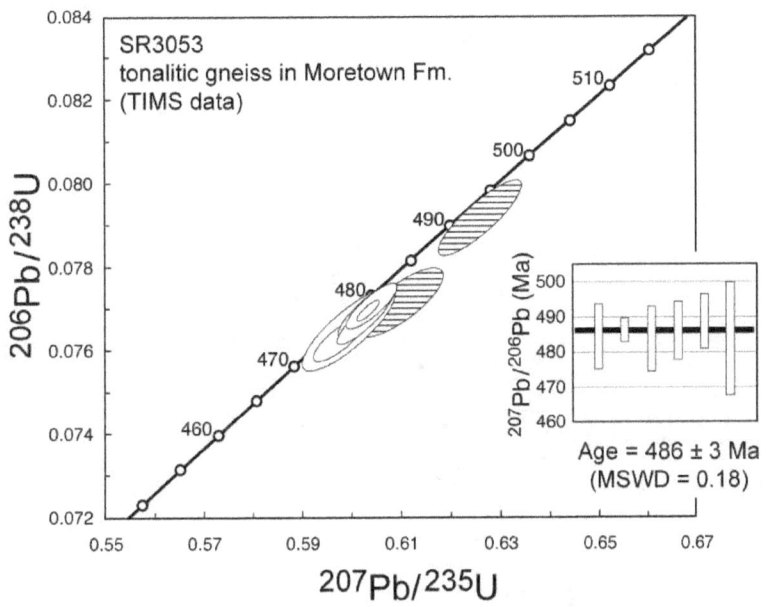

Figure 17. Conventional concordia plot of TIMS U-Pb data for zircon from tonalite gneiss in the North River Igneous Suite near Bartonsville, Vermont. Because data are nearly concordant with no spread, a best-fit regression was not calculated. Age, determined by calculating the weighted average of $^{207}Pb/^{206}Pb$ ages (n=6), is the time of igneous emplacement. Horizontally ruled ellipses represent older age (approx. 504 Ma) in cores from inherited zircon. Abbreviations are as follows: approx., approximately; Fm., Formation; km, kilometers; m, meters; Ma, millions of years (mega-annum); MSWD, mean square of the weighted deviates; SHRIMP, sensitive high resolution ion microprobe; WGS 84, World Geodetic System datum of 1984.

Sample number: 25
Description: Felsic volcanic layer interlayered with mafic volcanic rocks in the Cram Hill Formation at Springfield
Field number: SP450
Method: SHRIMP
Age: 483±3 Ma
Sample location coordinates (WGS 84 datum): 43°21'58"N., 72°28'47"W.
Sample location description: Sample collected from an outcrop about 2.8 km north-northeast of North Springfield Reservoir, about 1.2 km west of Weathersfield Center Road, in the Springfield quadrangle.

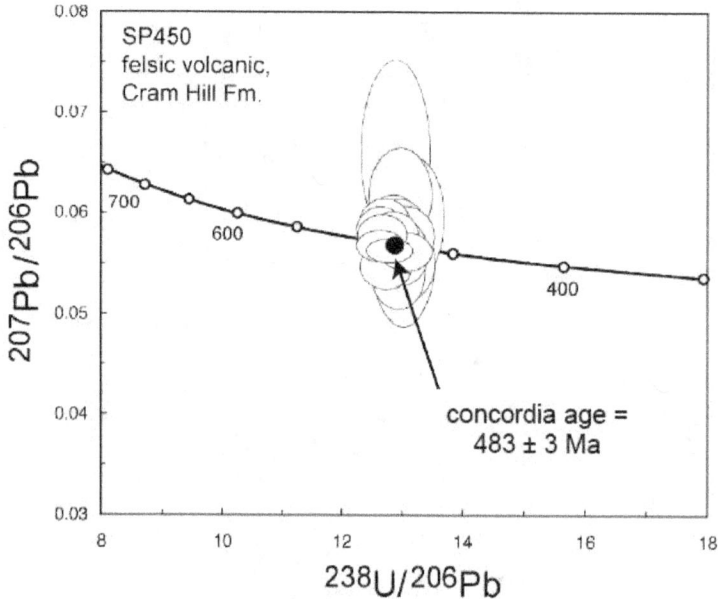

Figure 18. Tera-Wasserburg concordia plot of SHRIMP U-Pb data for zircon from felsic volcanic layer within mafic volcanic rocks in the Cram Hill Formation at Springfield, Vermont. Concordia age, calculated for data from oscillatory-zoned cores represented by white-filled error ellipses (*n*=20), is the time of volcanic crystallization. Abbreviations are as follows: Fm., Formation; km, kilometers; Ma, millions of years (mega-annum); SHRIMP, sensitive high resolution ion microprobe; WGS 84, World Geodetic System datum of 1984.

Sample number: 38
Description: Granite in the Braintree Intrusive Complex
Field number: MC3432
Method: SHRIMP
Age: 421±7 Ma
Sample location coordinates (WGS 84 datum): 43°59'56"N., 72°41'59"W.
Sample location description: Abandoned quarry on a trail on the western side of Ferry Hill, about 600 m north of Mud Pond, in the Randolph quadrangle.

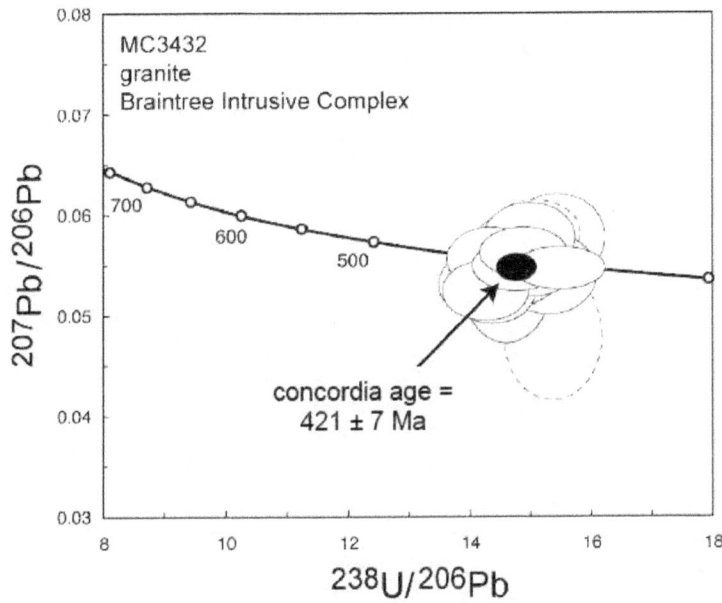

Figure 19. Tera-Wasserburg concordia plot of SHRIMP U-Pb data for zircon from granite in the Braintree Intrusive Complex, Vermont. Concordia age, calculated for data from oscillatory-zoned cores represented by white-filled error ellipses (n=14), is the time of igneous emplacement. Two slightly discordant analyses (dashed outlines of error ellipses) excluded from age calculation suggest minor lead loss. Abbreviations are as follows: m, meters; Ma, millions of years (mega-annum); SHRIMP, sensitive high resolution ion microprobe; WGS 84, World Geodetic System datum of 1984.

Sample number: 39
Description: Trondhjemite of the Newport Intrusive Complex
Field number: VT–Nq–1–97
Method: SHRIMP
Age: 425±3 Ma
Sample location coordinates (WGS 84 datum): 44°59′19″N., 72°14′43″W.
Sample location description: Outcrop on the southwestern side of Lake Road, west of Maxfield Point and south of Maxfield Point Road in Newport.

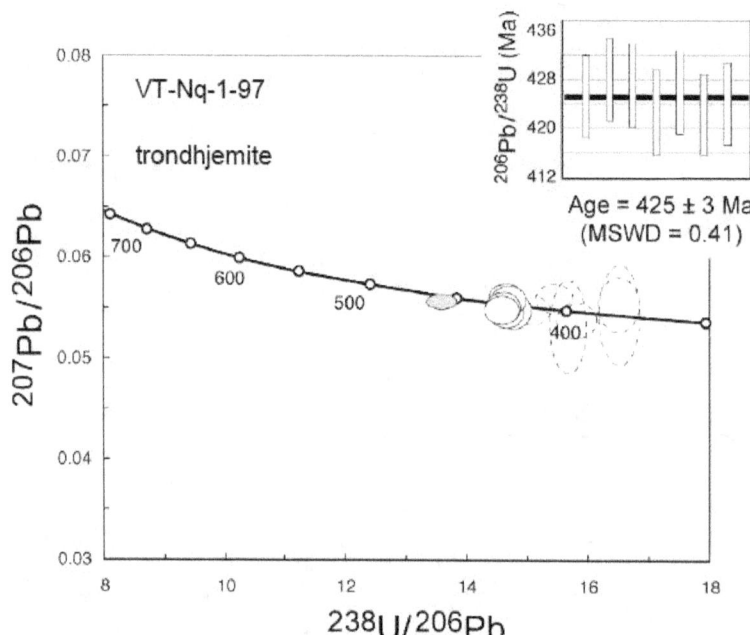

Figure 20. Tera-Wasserburg concordia plot of SHRIMP U-Pb data for zircon from trondhjemite of the Newport Intrusive Complex, Vermont. White-filled error ellipses represent data from oscillatory-zoned cores used in the weighted average calculation of ^{206}Pb/^{238}U ages (see inset) for determining the time of igneous emplacement. Discordant analyses (dashed outlines of error ellipses) caused by lead loss due to both somewhat high uranium concentrations (636–1,718 ppm; table 3) and cracked, deformed grains. Pale-gray error ellipse represents an older ^{206}Pb/^{238}U age that is due to a very high uranium concentration (2,852 ppm; table 3), which caused matrix effects (Williams and Hergt, 2000) that resulted in an inaccurate analysis. Abbreviations are as follows: Ma, millions of years (mega-annum); ppm, parts per million; MSWD, mean square of the weighted deviates; SHRIMP, sensitive high resolution ion microprobe; WGS 84, World Geodetic System datum of 1984.

Sample number: 46
Description: Granite in the Chester dome
Field number: VT–CSTR–2
Method: SHRIMP
Age: 392±6 Ma
Sample location coordinates (WGS 84 datum): 43°19'53"N., 72°35'06"W.
Sample location description: Small abandoned quarry east of Dean Brook Road, about 300 m north of Vermont Route 10, in the Chester quadrangle.

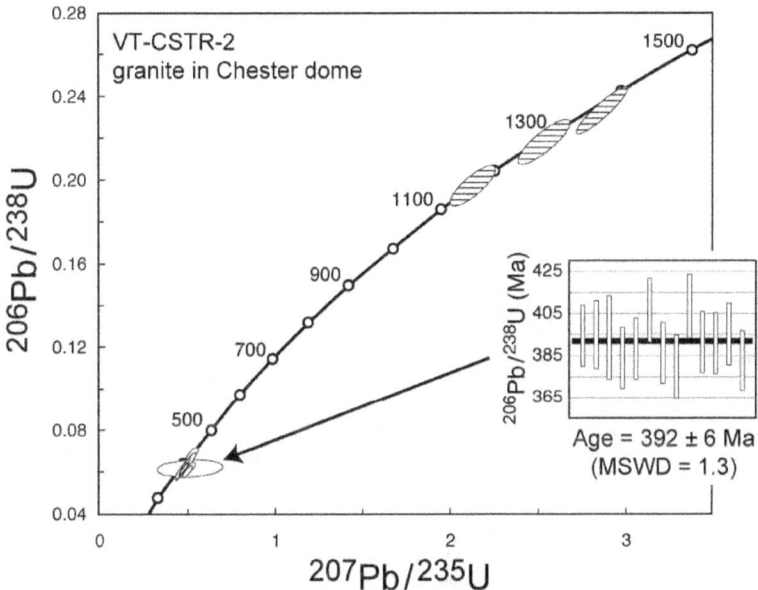

Figure 21. Conventional concordia plot of SHRIMP U-Pb data for zircon from granite in the Chester dome, Vermont. White-filled error ellipses represent data from oscillatory-zoned cores used in the weighted average calculation of $^{206}Pb/^{238}U$ ages (see inset) for determining the time of igneous emplacement. Horizontally ruled ellipses represent older ages (approx. 1.17, 1.29, 1.37 Ga) in cores from inherited zircon. Abbreviations are as follows: approx., approximately; Ga, billions of years (giga-annum); m, meters; Ma, millions of years (mega-annum); MSWD, mean square of the weighted deviates; SHRIMP, sensitive high resolution ion microprobe; WGS 84, World Geodetic System datum of 1984.

Sample number: 47
Description: Barre Granite at Rock of Ages quarry
Field number: Barre#2
Method: SHRIMP
Age: 368±4 Ma
Sample location coordinates (WGS 84 datum): 44°09′17″N., 72°28′50″W.
Sample location description: Rock of Ages quarry, main pit at the 11th-level deep, Barre.

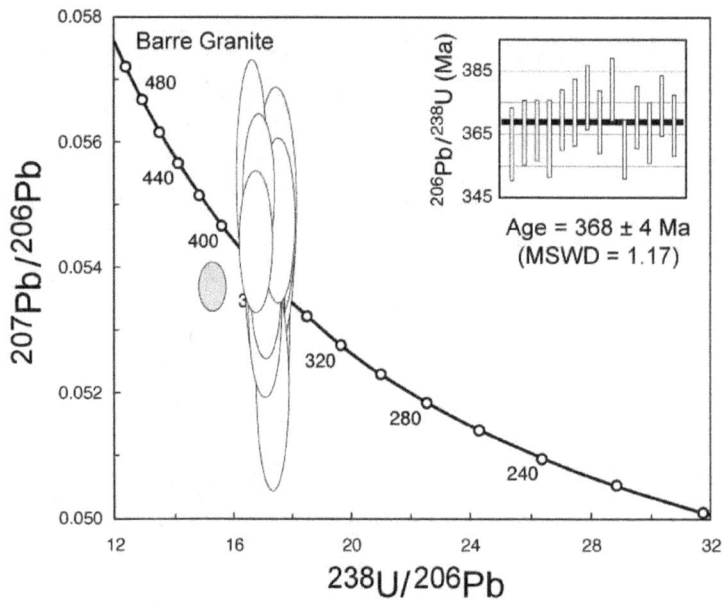

Figure 22. Tera-Wasserburg concordia plot of SHRIMP U-Pb data for zircon from Barre Granite, Rock of Ages quarry, Barre, Vermont. White-filled error ellipses represent data from oscillatory-zoned cores used in the weighted average calculation of $^{206}Pb/^{238}U$ ages (see inset) for determining the time of igneous emplacement. Pale-gray error ellipse represents an older $^{206}Pb/^{238}U$ age that is due to a very high uranium concentration (18,759 ppm; table 3), which caused matrix effects (Williams and Hergt, 2000) that resulted in an inaccurate analysis. Abbreviations are as follows: Ma, millions of years (mega-annum); MSWD, mean square of the weighted deviates; ppm, parts per million; SHRIMP, sensitive high resolution ion microprobe; WGS 84, World Geodetic System datum of 1984.

Sample number: 48
Description: Black Mountain pluton
Field number: VT/Br 1–89
Method: SHRIMP
Age: 364±4 Ma
Sample location coordinates (WGS 84 datum): 42°55′31″N., 72°36′33″W.
Sample location description: Abandoned quarry on the western slope of Black Mountain, due east from West Dummerston across the West River.

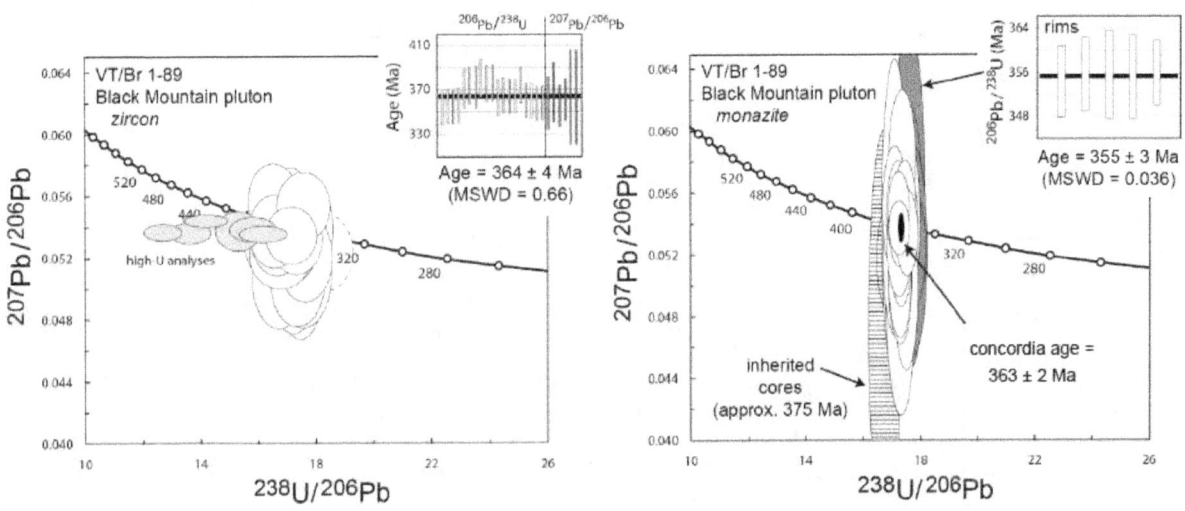

Figure 23. Tera-Wasserburg concordia plot of SHRIMP U-Pb data for zircon and monazite from the Black Mountain pluton, Vermont. In plot to left (zircon data), white-filled error ellipses represent data from low-uranium oscillatory-zoned cores; pale-gray error ellipses represent older $^{206}Pb/^{238}U$ ages that are due to a very high uranium concentration (10,177–30,266 ppm; table 3), which caused matrix effects (Williams and Hergt, 2000) that resulted in inaccurate analyses. Age was determined by (1) calculating the weighted average of the low-uranium $^{206}Pb/^{238}U$ ages, (2) calculating the weighted average of the high-uranium $^{207}Pb/^{206}Pb$ ages, (3) calculating a combined weighted average of the ages from (1) and (2) (see inset). This age was interpreted as the time of igneous emplacement. In plot to right (monazite data), the concordia age was calculated for data from sector-zoned cores, represented by white-filled error ellipses (n=23). The age agrees with the zircon SHRIMP U-Pb age. Gray-filled ellipses (n=5) represent data from unzoned rims, suggesting a slightly younger, post-crystallization thermal event. Slightly older ages of about 375 Ma, represented by two horizontally ruled error ellipses, may be due to inheritance. Abbreviations are as follows: approx., approximately; Ma, millions of years (mega-annum); MSWD, mean square of the weighted deviates; ppm, parts per million; SHRIMP, sensitive high resolution ion microprobe; WGS 84, World Geodetic System datum of 1984.

Sample number: 49
Description: Granite dike south of Plymouth
Field number: VT/Pl 2–91
Method: SHRIMP
Age: 365±5 Ma
Sample location coordinates (WGS 84 datum): 43°30'14"N., 72°43'23"W.
Sample location description: The sampled outcrop is located in the western part of a sand pit about 170 m east of Vermont Route 100, and about 150 m north-northeast of the junction of Frog City Road and Route 100.

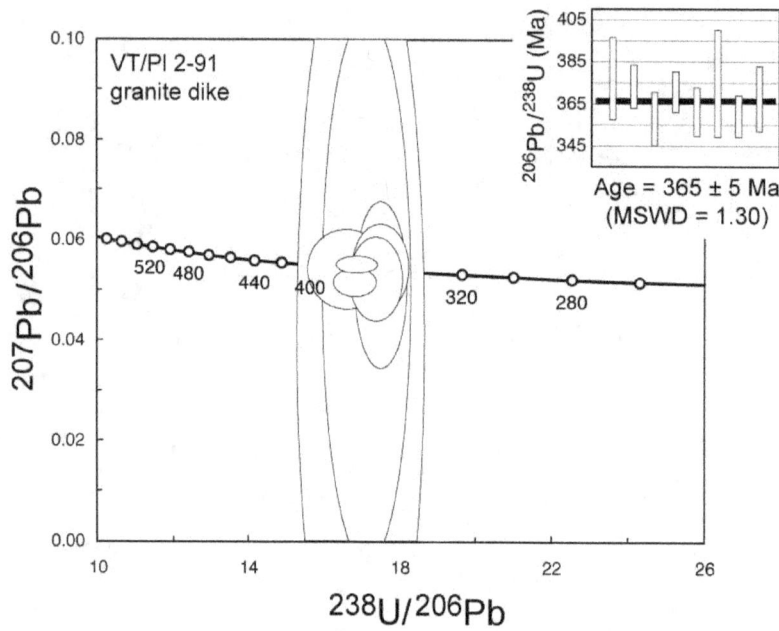

Figure 24. Tera-Wasserburg concordia plot of SHRIMP U-Pb data for zircon from a granite dike near Plymouth, Vermont. White-filled error ellipses represent data from oscillatory-zoned cores used in the weighted average calculation of ^{206}Pb/^{238}U ages (see inset) for determining the time of igneous emplacement. Abbreviations are as follows: m, meters; Ma, millions of years (mega-annum); MSWD, mean square of the weighted deviates; ppm, parts per million; SHRIMP, sensitive high resolution ion microprobe; WGS 84, World Geodetic System datum of 1984.

www.ingramcontent.com/pod-product-compliance
Lightning Source LLC
Chambersburg PA
CBHW080341290526
45791CB00009BA/2685